POSTMODERNITY

GUIDES TO THEOLOGICAL INQUIRY

Edited by Kathryn Tanner of the University of Chicago and Paul Lakeland of Fairfield University, *Guides to Theological Inquiry* are intended to introduce students, scholars, clergy, and theologians to those academic methods, disciplines, and movements that are most germane to contemporary theology. Neither simple surveys nor exhaustive monographs, these short books will provide solid, reliable, programmatic statements of the main lines or workings of their topics and assessments of their theological impact.

Already available are *Nonfoundationalism* by John E. Thiel, *Literary Theory* by David Dawson, *Postmodernity* by Paul Lakeland, and *Theories of Culture* by Kathryn Tanner. Forthcoming titles in the series include *Hermeneutics* by Francis Schüssler Fiorenza, *Feminist Theory* by Serene Jones, *Critical Social Theory* by Gary Simpson, and *African American Critical Thought* by Shawn Copeland.

POSTMODERNITY

CHRISTIAN IDENTITY
IN A FRAGMENTED AGE

PAUL LAKELAND

GUIDES TO
THEOLOGICAL
INQUIRY

FORTRESS PRESS / MINNEAPOLIS

POSTMODERNITY
Christian Identity in a Fragmented Age
Guides to Theological Inquiry series

Cover design: Craig Claeys
Text design: David Lott
Cover photo: © 1997 Tony Stone Images
Author photo: Kevin Wolfthal

Library of Congress Cataloging-in-Publication Data

Lakeland, Paul, 1946–
    Postmodernity : Christian identity in a fragmented age / Paul Lakeland.
        p.   cm. — (Guides to theological inquiry)
    Includes bibliographical references and index.
    ISBN 0-8006-3098-X (alk. paper)
    1. Theology—Methodology. 2. Postmodernism—Religious aspects—Christianity. 3. Identification (Religion) 4. Christianity—20th century. I. Title. II. Series
    BR118.L25   1997
    230'.046—dc21   97-23817
                                        CIP

Manufactured in the U.S.A.   AF 1-3098

01   00   99   98   97   1   2   3   4   5   6   7   8   9   10

Contents

For Jonathan Palmer Lakeland
who, if he ever reads any of this,
will do so in the age that follows
postmodernity

Foreword

No self-sufficient enterprise, Christian theology always proceeds in intellectual dialogue with other forms of inquiry. Perhaps a habit fostered by chance in the Hellenistic milieu in which Christianity achieved its greatest initial success, perhaps a necessary outcome of its desire to speak from a Christian point of view about the whole of life—whatever the reason—theology had philosophy as its dialogue partner from the first and for much of its history. With the contraction, however, of philosophy's scope in the late nineteenth century and the parceling out of its domain to the disciplines of the modern academy (economics, politics, psychology, and so forth), the theologian's task of keeping up this dialogue became more difficult. The aim of the *Guides to Theological Inquiry* series is to help ease this burden by familiarizing people with major academic movements and disciplines and by clarifying the ways in which they might be of continuing importance for theological investigation.

Postmodernity is a thread running through new directions being taken in a number of academic fields covered by this series. Without the confusion and obfuscation that mar so many academic treatments of this crucial topic, Paul Lakeland firmly anchors the discussion of postmodernity in the character of experience in today's world. With great wit and theological insight he lays out the way postmodern questions about subjectivity, moral pluralism, and respect for "otherness" challenge theologians to rethink their understandings of God, church, and Christ. A rich and suggestive final chapter outlines the way a constructive apologetic theology might meaningfully address a postmodern world.

—*Kathryn Tanner*

Preface

This book is about two facets of Christianity in today's world. It explores, in the first place, how the so-called postmodern character of our contemporary culture affects the religious tradition and how that tradition can meaningfully address such a postmodern world. Second, it examines the significance of postmodern thought for religion and the impact of postmodern intellectual currents upon the practice of theology. To put it another way, this work is one more book about "religion today," but this time the subject is approached on the understanding that the "postmodern" label accurately depicts today's world and thus, when understood, informs the agenda for religion and theology. And so we shall have to begin by examining the language of the postmodernity debate and the reality that the word *postmodern* claims to denote.

Ours is a world that, for better or worse, has been labeled "postmodern." What that label may mean is obviously something we must try to determine at the outset of our enterprise. One might, of course, argue that in using the word *postmodern* to describe our world, we have begged the question of its usefulness. Once used, it has to be explained. While there might be some truth in this charge, there is also a defense. However unsatisfactory and ill-defined it may be, it has almost become a commonplace to call our world postmodern. As a consequence, those of us who live in this world and—as religious people, students of religion, and theologians—take it seriously, need to address the reality to which the word refers, even if we detest the word itself.

While we are probably stuck, for the moment, with the terminology of postmodernism, there is no attendant clarity about the *meaning* of that terminology. There are probably a thousand different self-appointed commentators on the postmodern phenomenon[1] and bewildering discrepancies between the ways many of these authors understand the term *postmodern* and its cognates. If, in this brief book, even a tenth of them were considered, there would be no room to address the book's real purpose. At the same time, if *no* theories or theorists were introduced, the reader would be unable to recognize the location of this particular book in the jungle of postmodern analysis. Thus, while these pages include no formal or extended taxonomy of the postmodern phenomenon, we must of necessity begin by acquiring a sense of the range of interpretive possibilities. Only then can the use of the terms in this present book make any real sense.

A recital of a number of competing and overlapping issues and questions may illustrate the complexity of the postmodernity debate. Is the "post" in postmodern(ity), for example, sheerly an indication that the postmodern is the cultural/historical epoch that follows the modern, or is the "post" taken to indicate a continuing relationship to modernity? If the latter, is that relationship adversarial, or filial, or both? Does postmodern stand in the same relationship to modern as post-Christian to Christian, as postgraduate to undergraduate, or as postcoital to coition? Is it essentially rejection, succession, or a relaxed if bathetic afterglow? What is the relationship between postmodern architecture and postmodern philosophy? And how is postmodernity, with its characteristic celebration of pop culture, related to neoconservatism? Is it, as we might initially suspect, anathema to neoconservatives, or might not neoconservatism forge an alliance with postmodernity against the common enemy, the critical spirit of modernity? Is the relationship postmodernity/postmodernism parallel to that of modernity/modernism? Is postmodernism really "the end of the master narratives" (Jean-François Lyotard) or "the effort to take the temperature of the age without instruments and in a situation in which we are not even sure there is so coherent a thing as an 'age' or *zeitgeist* or 'system' or 'current situation' any longer" (Fredric Jameson)? Is it "that heterogeneous range of lifestyles and language games which has renounced the nostalgic urge to totalize and legitimate itself" (Terry Eagleton)? Is it "a rage against humanism and the Enlightenment legacy" (Richard Bernstein)? Or is it merely "the cultural logic of late capitalism" (Jameson again)?[2]

Commentators on postmodernism seem to be in agreement that there are at least two different forms of engagement with it, although there is not at all as much consensus on how to describe them. Hal Foster, for example, talks of a postmodernism of resistance and a postmodernism of reaction. The one "seeks to deconstruct modernism and resist the status quo," while the other "repudiates the former to celebrate the latter."[3] Andreas Huyssen does something similar, identifying critical and affirmative varieties of postmodernism.[4] David Harvey's ambivalent attitude to postmodernism leads him to distinguish between what he sees as its laudable skepticism about totalizing modes of discourse on the one hand, and its deplorable incapacity to assume any political posture on the other.[5] Alex Callinicos finds postmodernism at the confluence of three converging rivers: the architectural revolt against the "International Style," poststructuralist theory, and a theory of postindustrial society.[6] Finally (at least for now), Stephen White enumerates four phenomena that he believes to be the essential postmodern issues: growing incredulity toward traditional metanarratives, new awareness of the costs of societal rationalization, the explosion of informational technologies, and the emergence of new social movements.[7]

Much of the confusion with which the debate about the postmodern is frequently bedeviled is often negotiated by the observation that there are two postmodernisms, and that postmodernity itself is a dialectical reality. This assertion follows first from the recognition that "modernity" is a term that we may use to label two quite distinct phenomena. One is the modernism of late nineteenth- and twentieth-century art, architecture, and literature; the other is the modern world of reason, science, and technological progress ushered in by the Enlightenment. Second, we have to determine whether we are dealing with a critical confrontation with one or other form of the modern, or some response that is essentially in continuity, if highly intensified or somehow refocused, with modernity's spirit and objectives. Finally, we need to allow the rigid distinctions to be collapsed, to see that in the end the aesthetic and the sociopolitical are always going to impinge upon and often to be closely engaged with one another.[8] So, for example, postmodern architecture's rejection of the inhuman scale of modernist buildings is not far removed in spirit from the devolutionary impulses of postmodern political organizing.

While this assertion of two forms of postmodernism is helpful, it does not go far enough. There are, in fact, many forms of the postmodern, each in some way a comment upon the modern. Counting on the fingers of one hand, a number spring immediately to mind. There is first the poststructuralist intensification of modernist cultural impulses, then the eclectic reprise of premodern artistic themes and styles, coupled most frequently with a deliberate collapse of the distinction between so-called high culture and popular culture. Third, there is the appropriation of the Enlightenment spirit to move beyond the perceived inhumanity of late capitalist society, and fourth there is the radical rejection of the white male Enlightenment master narrative. Fifth, there is a nostalgic postmodernism, really a "countermodernism" in disguise, which seeks to undo the harm of the modern and—at least in its religious dress—build a series of New Jerusalems or Cities of God within the contemporary world.

While we will have a certain amount to say in the course of these pages about the "affirmative" or celebratory kind of postmodernism, our focus will be on its critical and oppositional character. Here its potential is directly reflective of the accuracy of its critiques of what went before, above all, its challenge to the legacy of the Enlightenment. The Enlightenment consolidated a belief in the inviolability of the Cartesian ego, put its faith in human reason as the power of mastery over nature and fate, and thus created the intellectual conditions for the explosion of science and technology—the individual's application of reason in order to subdue nature. Postmodernism is a frontal attack on all of this. It abandons the idea of ordered progress toward some goal, in which the autonomous human subject exercises the power of reason to subdue and arrange previously intractable nature toward that end. It is deeply suspicious of notions of universal reason, and it rejects all metaphysical or religious foundations, all "grand theory," all theoretical systems.

We are, as the reader can now see, dealing with a somewhat complicated terminological background. It will be simplified, however, in the following way throughout the ensuing pages. First, "postmodernity" will be employed here as a nonjudgmental, purely descriptive term to evoke today's world. While most of what makes our world is inherited from the past, that which renders it postmodern is novelty. Postmodernity is then constituted by the interplay between the given and the novel. These novel elements, we shall determine descriptively, display certain common characteristics, affects, and impulses that will license usage of the term *postmodern*. Second, "postmodern thought" is a term that will be used for writing that engages these novel cultural developments. Some such postmodern thought, of course, denies the reality of postmodernity or—more frequently—insists that it is simply the latest phase of modernism (a point of view that has much in its favor). But the greater part of the corpus of writing either embraces postmodernity or engages it creatively and critically. On the whole, the term "*postmodernism*" will be avoided, since outside the visual arts, where it may be justified, it suggests a misleading sense of a school or theoretical movement. Postmodern thought, on the contrary, mirrors in its multiplicity of forms, ideologies, and agendas the playful eclecticism of postmodernity itself.[9]

The book is divided into three chapters. Chapter 1 begins by describing the salient characteristics of postmodernity. It identifies the postmodern elements in our contemporary world as manifestations in one way or another of the breakdown in previously fundamental coordinates of experience: time, space, and order. This very thorough undermining of old certainties, while creating as much anxiety as any significant historical shift would do, is connected to a distinctly postmodern sensibility, characterized by cheerful ahistoricality, contented rootlessness, guiltless consumerism, and low expectations of the future. What is not clear is the degree to which the sensibility is a product of the cultural shift, or the cultural shift a reflection of the new sensibility. The chapter next turns to those forms of contemporary philosophy, social theory, and cultural criticism that have an impact on our capacity to understand the phenomenon of postmodernity. In this section we shall consider the range of attitudes within postmodern thought to the legacy of philosophical modernity, as they influence three specific philosophical questions: the inquiry into subjectivity and its nature, the issue of ethical pluralism and relativism in a postmetaphysical age, and the sociopolitical implications of confronting "otherness." The chapter concludes with a brief note on postmodern science.

Chapter 2 looks at different facets of the interconnections between postmodernity and religion. It first examines in some detail a theological correlate to the philosophical problem of subjectivity, namely, the postmodern reconceptualization of "God." Then it turns to the issue of the role of the Christian communities in a morally pluralistic society;

and finally it considers the question of otherness in a specifically theological issue, the relationship between Christianity and other religious traditions. The third and final chapter is a more constructive attempt to outline a theological apologetics for the postmodern world. Taking up once again the issues of subjectivity, relativism, and otherness in their theological exemplars of God, church, and Christ, this chapter examines the mission of the church to the postmodern world and the kinds of ways in which basic theological symbols can and cannot participate in that mission. It is here in the traditional subdiscipline of apologetics, I will argue, that the theological tradition and the postmodern world must meet; and while the initiative for this meeting lies in the tradition's sense of mission, the language to be used is very definitely that of the world. Apologetics is unapologetically "the moment of mediation."

It is always a pleasure to be able to recognize the debts we owe to others, professional, social, and domestic. This work owes much to a variety of people and undoubtedly owes at least something to many of my students, whose remarks on one thing or another will have caused me to say one or another thing in these pages. But as I cannot for the life of me connect any particular student with any particular remark, the thanks is both heartfelt and impersonal.

First among those I can thank by name are J. Michael West and David Lott of Fortress Press and Kathryn Tanner, my coeditor on this series and editor for this particular volume. They have been as collegial, helpful, and congenial as one could possibly hope for. To my colleague and friend John Thiel I owe the by-now-customary debt of gratitude for encouragement and close reading of the text. Additionally, I have to thank other colleagues for reading all or part of the text in progress, and making many helpful comments. Nancy Dallavalle, Dennis Keenan, and Beth Newman were particularly helpful in this regard. I am grateful too to the members of the Faculty Research Colloquium at Fairfield University who engaged in a spirited discussion of an earlier draft of part of this work, and to Fairfield University for a sabbatical leave in 1994 that enabled me at least to begin to draft out the present work. Above all I am thankful for the support of my wife, Beth Palmer, and for the companionship of my son Jonathan, to whom this work is dedicated, in sublime disregard for whether he will, one day, actually read any of it.

1

Postmodernity

The Culture of Postmodernity

Each venture is a new beginning, a raid on the inarticulate.
—T. S. Eliot

Postmodernity, as I suggested in the Preface, is constituted by the interplay between the given and the novel. It is in the air we breathe, and the semantic implications of "postmodernity" mislead us if we think the word itself contains meaning. It is a way of saying "our time, not some other." But, of course, our time both reacts and takes an attitude to the time that went before, just as it may also hark back nostalgically to the recent or distant past and probably looks forward, in hope or dread, to a time to come. What makes it this moment in history, and not some other, is its difference from what went before, not its similarities, though the latter will in all probability outnumber the former. And the novel is always, of course, relational to that which it supersedes. Consciously or unconsciously, the present moment takes an attitude toward the preceding time. It may improve upon it, abandon it, transform it, castigate it, but it cannot simply repeat it. Then it would not be the novel, for the novel, of its nature, is noticeable.

At the outset of this chapter I want to sketch some of the more noticeable features of cultural postmodernity, without praise or blame. Analysis and critique will follow later, but our task for the moment is simply to draw attention to novel elements in our own world. Obviously, this project must be heavily circumscribed, or it will simply never end. Like *Tristram Shandy*, the events of the moment will outstrip the capacities of the recorder, and we shall fall further and further behind. I propose, accordingly, to restrict myself first to a description of some of the salient characteristics of life in late-twentieth-century, late-capitalist societies, trying to capture the quality of the times and, second, to an attempt to describe the attendant postmodern sensibility. Of course, one of the most obvious characteristics of postmodernity is the degree to which a world culture is coming into existence, as a result above all of the explosion in information technologies. Consequently, much of what will be described is true way beyond the confines of "our" society, but apart from noting that this is so, we cannot attend to it further. Similarly, there are all kinds of possible nuances in a socioeconomic consideration of the impact of postmodernity. Middle- and upper-class Americans are perhaps more likely to be practitioners of a postmodern sensibility and be more at home in postmodern culture than their less-affluent or less-educated fellow citizens, who may at times be rightly perceived as victims of these same cultural currents. But while it is not as simple as that—true popular culture, for example, is an important phenomenon within postmodernity—this too is a concern that would lead to a loss of focus in the present work, and must be laid aside.

My organizing assumption, for the originality of which I make no claims, is that the postmodern elements in our contemporary world are all manifestations in one way or another of a breakdown of what have previously been taken to be "givens," fundamental coordinates of experience. The givens in question are time, space, and order. Postmodernity puts each of these three into question, both collapsing and then expanding the understanding of each.

To begin on the safest if not the most startling grounds, let us consider some of the implications of postmodern architecture for our sense of time, space, and order. It was in architecture that the language of the postmodern was first used, and it is in the bricks and mortar, wood and stone of buildings and monuments that we can best feel the difference between what has been around for a while, and what has not. Very few of us, I am sure, react negatively to, say, a Greek temple, a Gothic cathedral, an ivy-clad Oxford college, a Bavarian rococo church, or a white clapboard New England chapel. Very many of us, I am equally willing to venture, have distinctly negative feelings about high-rise public housing, or the extensive postwar real-estate subdivisions of Pete Seeger's "little boxes, little boxes, little boxes on the hillside, and they're all made out of ticky-tacky, and they all look just the same." Whether it's Co-op City in the Bronx or the outskirts of Stalinist Warsaw, Moscow, or Ulan Bator, we tend to shun the massively inhuman architecture that represents, as a Polish Communist Party official once privately confessed to me, "the triumph of ideology over common sense." In this distaste for the recent past's architectural accomplishments, and comfort with the artifacts of an earlier time, we are all potentially postmodernists. And, when we admit to ourselves that we cannot simply go back, we come even closer. The postmodern is the simultaneous cancellation and preservation of the past (the Hegelian *Aufhebung* or "sublation," as Fredric Jameson has suggested), but in architecture at least it seems bent on the cancellation of modernism and the preservation—though subtly changed—of what went before.

Postmodern architecture is distinguished by its playfulness, its historical allusions and stylistic eclecticism, and, more seriously, by its rejection of the inhuman scale and utopian pretensions of architectural modernism. It is both good and bad, and we find it, good and bad alike, in expensive architect-designed private homes, but also in public spaces, especially in shopping malls and hotels. All the forms of postmodern architecture, public and private, use modern materials, often at least appearing to be prefabricated or unfinished, while echoing or referring to elements of previous architectural styles and their solid, classical materials (so, marble or leather embellishments of glass and chrome), sometimes even enclosing one within another in a practice known as "wrapping."

As has often been remarked, the shopping mall takes the old downtown and puts the outside inside, even down to fountains, trees, and "outdoor" cafes. "Sidewalk sales" occur inside. And since within the air-conditioned environment of the mall the need for doors to stores is not there, the inside also becomes the outside! The postmodern hotel[1] concentrates its attention on vast internal public spaces, shutting out the outside world, creating a kind of city in miniature. Many of them incorporate shopping malls within their space, and almost all banish the original intent of hotels—that is, to provide comfortable lodging—to a series of undistinguished and indistinguishable boxes built high up around the periphery of the building. Rooms most often look into the inner concourse, not out onto the street, and elevators made of glass slide quietly up and down the walls of the public space. Entrances are few and often difficult to locate, and finding your way from floor to floor, where elevators and moving staircases are positioned in seemingly random and inconvenient fashion, is, as any frequent traveler knows, the first challenge after checking in. Most characteristically, while the spaces themselves may be quite vast, the human response to them is usually to smile; they delight and amuse, they do not overwhelm. And I have never, to my knowledge, seen a clock in one of these public spaces, designed as they are to eradicate the distinction between night and day.

Even considering the phenomenon of postmodern architecture so briefly, it is easy enough to see that it challenges many of our basic assumptions about time, space, and order. The hotel or shopping mall or house or housing complex that is self-consciously postmodern calls attention to itself as an artificially created world apart. Its signs and symbols deliberately deny any connection either to the natural world, or to the "ordinary" world of urban spaces in which its beholders inevitably, in fact, continue to live. Perhaps this is why the quintessentially postmodern space is devoted either to time away from ordinary life (the hotel) or to the principal leisure-time activity of today (shopping). Equally, it sidesteps the natural and inherited senses of time. Daylight is unimportant, the climate is controlled, and you can shop furiously at ten o'clock at night. Nothing is old, worn, weather-beaten, mellowed with age; age is the enemy. Look in a shopping mall for antique stores, consignment stores, stores catering to the tastes and figures of the older population. Look in the hotel for a library, a reading room, even a closed-off space where you can take tea or just relax. You will look in vain. And again, and largely because of what these places do to notions of space and time, another order than the one we inherited is subtly instilled: the order of commodification, buttressed by the ubiquity of the charge card. The artificiality of the environment affects consciousness, and spending becomes easier, occurring as it does in a space and time unrelated to the everyday realities of bank accounts, budgets, and "payment overdue" notices. Architecture leads into changes in consciousness, even perhaps produces such changes, and the changes connect to those bottom-line realities of our world, marketing and sales.

Many other facets of life today are susceptible to just the same sort of analysis. The computer, for example, challenges notions of time, space, and order, in its remarkable speed, increasing miniaturization, and creation of all kinds of possibilities for modeling alternate realities and producing, indeed, "virtual reality," perhaps that most postmodern of all developments. In virtual reality, you can experience the phenomenon without going there, being there, or interacting with another living soul. And even the business of drugs, with its connections between alternate reality, marketing, leisure, and the destruction of inherited patterns of time, space, and order, has its claim to be a postmodern phenomenon.

The postmodern does not stop at the boundaries of artificially created public spaces. It also increasingly permeates domestic spaces, even those which—like most—show no trace of architectural postmodernism in their construction. If we took a look around a sample of modern, middle-class households we would surely find, quite quickly, examples of all of the following: microcomputers with games that approach the creation of virtual reality, or with modems that annihilate the space between the house and the worksite, or the house and the bank; the World Wide Web; large-screen televisions equipped with "surround sound"; trees in the house and furniture in the garden, or domestic spaces that play with the ambiguous nature of the distinction between the inside and the outside; freezers full of microwaveable foods; extensive video libraries; cathedral ceilings with skylights, and walls with picture windows; quantities of clothing that is desirable because of the label *on the outside* ("Guess," "Gucci," "Burberry," or "Ralph Lauren"), or because of what it advertises on front or back, or because it is new but looks old (designer-ripped, "distressed," or prefaded); luxury cars that stress how well the outside is kept out while the CD player brings you Vivaldi, new-age eclecticism, or hard rock. All of these developments, in their own ways, celebrate or demonstrate the collapse of time, the reconfiguration of space, the redefinition of order.

Some postmodern developments are or at least seem to be relatively harmless, while others are truly threatening. Much of what we have said about architecture, for example, is playful and even delightful in its impact on the human senses, and the same can certainly be said for the products of the contemporary fashion industry. If even half of what is said about the commodification of the environment is true, however, then the apparently harmless may still give us pause for thought, may even verge upon the sinister. Take the "Swatch" phenomenon, for example. Developed a dozen or so years ago, the Swatch was conceived as a wristwatch with interchangeable bands and surrounds for the clockface, made of the cheapest materials, and sold for a few dollars. In many cases, they were designed specifically for and given away as part of promotions for other products. They were fashion gimmicks, throwaway products, and throw them away is exactly what many owners did as they tired of them, or wanted gold, or as they wore out. How sorry they are now, as these same cheap or free watches in some cases fetch ten or twenty or even thirty thousand dollars! The small, relatively new, essentially inexpensive plastic object is now extremely valuable only because of its scarcity. There is no great artistry or some splendid technological feat that is being valued here. The Swatch, in its scarcity, celebrates a marketing concept. And this, for good or ill, certainly suggests a shifting scale of values.

So much of our world could be subjected to this kind of consideration, but since both your author and his publisher live in a postmodern world, there is neither space nor time. And, as surely as you are not reading this book in fine leather binding with beautiful endpapers, just as surely would you not welcome the multiple volumes that the vastness of the subject demands. So let us proceed with a rather breathless listing of some of the further phenomena and ephemera that merit consideration here. Take aging and death, for example. For all of human history people have dreamed about the extension of life or at least of youth. Today, technology and capitalism go hand in hand to provide for those who can afford it, cosmetic surgery, anti-wrinkle creams, and in the end, cryogenics. In high modernity, we fantasized about Dracula's undead and Frankenstein's monster. Colorful brochures now offer the merits of freeze-drying the not-yet-dead, decapitating them and storing the heads for a new life in a disease- and death-free future. Medical technology and organ transplants bring the moment of the bionic person ever closer.

On a less macabre note, consider the effect on consciousness of the new communications technologies. The fax machine collapses space and time, and I can order my lunch, do my shopping, send a letter, or submit a manuscript instantaneously, even in hard copy. The Internet is only beginning to transform the home and the workplace. Worldwide

CNN simultaneously brings us all to the battlefront and puts us at the mercy of news editors for our perception of reality. The growth of international terrorism brings us into even greater proximity to the world's flash points. We may, if we are lucky or venal or both, ride to work in the sealed environment of our Infiniti, but we could all be blown at any moment into another kind of infinity, by someone we neither know nor have ever seen, nor whose predicament we understand, but whose brothers and sisters were brought into our living room every day of the previous year, courtesy of cable TV.

To take a somewhat different tack, our world is distinguished clearly from its immediate predecessor world of modernity by knowing so much more and expecting so much less. We could define and chart the rise and fall of modernity in terms of the fate of the idea of progress, from its unchallenged, almost unnoticed, axiomatic status in the heyday of the Industrial Revolution, through a twentieth century distinguished by a prodigality that testified to the continuing value of the myth of progress, to a present day when our immeasurably greater technological know-how has come into head-on confrontation with diminishing resources. Thus, postmodernity emerges, we might say, at the point at which we face the fact that know-how and can-do may not always any longer so smoothly interlock as perhaps they once did. We have the finest medical care, measured in terms of its technological capabilities, that has ever existed, but cancer and AIDS run amok, and tuberculosis is threatening a comeback. Even worse, the new viruses we are beginning to discover as we despoil the last stretches of virgin forest and meet species we have never encountered before threaten us with much greater catastrophe. We have the capability to build cities of such efficiency and even grace, yet the cities we already have are on the verge of collapse, threatened with levels of pollution that make breathing dangerous, and awash in quantities of urban violence that put the number of murder victims well ahead of those who succumb to asthma. Los Angeles and New York: so much money and talent and vitality, yet so much dirt, and so much death. Is postmodernity the dusk of modernity, in which Hegel's Owl of Minerva takes flight and counts the cost of the Enlightenment? Or is postmodernity "the dawning of the Age of Aquarius," when the true change—a change in consciousness—finally occurs?

The Postmodern Sensibility

Fleet the time carelessly, as they did in the golden world.
—William Shakespeare, *As You Like It*

Before we begin to investigate the kind of meaning-questions that I started to raise at the end of the last paragraph, we need to add to this lightning-sketch of the postmodern world a similarly brief account of the distinctive postmodern sensibility. Here we must tread more carefully. It is one thing to catalogue the novel elements in our culture, and while we may be accused of overlooking some elements and overvaluing others, there ought to be little dispute that what we have included, should be included. But who is to say *which* set of emotional and intellectual reactions to our world is "distinctively postmodern"? We might assume that it is postmodern to embrace postmodernity, but it equally well might be postmodern to recoil in horror from all that it portends. Perhaps a critical and even oppositional spirit is postmodern, or maybe we need to look to the channel surfer, riding the airwaves armed only with a six-pack, a bucket of popcorn, and a remote control. And it might be none or all of the above.

What is characteristic of the postmodern sensibility will not be discovered in the surface commitments of postmodernity but actually in what is active but submerged in the consciousness of most if not all of those alive today, whatever their professed attitude to the times in which we live. For that reason, if for no other, we may have to look deeper, to reach that layer of sensibility that its possessors may not even be aware they manifest. To provide a simple illustration from an earlier time, had we conducted a similar investigation in the second half of the nineteenth century, we should have found that most writers and artists, most historians and scientists, most industrialists and politicians and bishops, however different their respective worldviews, shared an unthematized optimism and an unconscious conviction that progress was a part of the natural order. What we need to identify are the parallel deep structures of the postmodern sensibility.

The postmodern sensibility, let me suggest, is nonsequential, noneschatological, nonutopian, nonsystematic, nonfoundational, and, ultimately, nonpolitical. The postmodern human being wants a lot but expects little. The emotional range is narrow, between mild depression at one end and a whimsical insouciance at the other. Postmodern heroes and heroines are safe, so far beyond that we could not possibly emulate them, avatars of power or success or money or sex—all without consequences. Who really expects to be like Arnold Schwarzenegger— probably the best-known and highest-paid actor in the world—or Madonna? Postmodernity may be tragic, but its denizens are unable to recognize tragedy. The shows we watch, the movies we see, the music we hear, all are devoted to a counterfactual presentation of life as comic, sentimental, and comfortable. Reality doesn't sell. So here we stand at the end of the twentieth century, a century that has seen two world wars, countless holocausts, the end of the myth of progress, and the near-death of hope, playing our computer games and whiling away the time with the toys that material success brings.

What may be sounding dangerously like the indictment of a genera- tion for triviality is at least as much the celebration of a critical posture. Postmodern human beings, in inchoate and unthematized ways, are reacting against the failure of the recent past, not simply hiding from an unwelcome reality. And in the precise form of their reactions may lie a clue to a path onward, if not exactly upward, that the sheer onwardness of time expects of us. Behind those negative characteristics of the post- modern sensibility listed above lurk their positive counterparts. So, the Sartrean despair that replaces eschatological hope is revealed to be a courageous and self-limiting fortitude. The order, sequence, and system that Nietzsche castigated as "aesthetic anthropomorphisms," a view that postmodernity embraces, are not, however, displaced by mere chaos. Instead, a virtuous delight in difference and otherness is cultivat- ed. The loss of faith in utopias and grand designs opens onto a more limited but achievable attention to local initiatives, tactical forays in the direction of a more human life in the here and now. Thus can the post- modern be both trivial and substantial at the same time. But the sub- stance, it would seem, rests upon the insubstantial. Marx's famous phrase, "all that is solid melts into air," is as true of postmodernity as it was of modernity.[2] The difference, again, seems to be that postmoder- nity's nose, unlike that of modernity, is not put out of joint by the real- ization that what can be achieved is really quite limited.

There are at least three distinguishable types of postmodern humanity, and here I must be forgiven broad brushstrokes. First, there is the *obvious*, at once the product and consumer of popular postmodern culture. Whether young (the so-called MTV generation), not-so-young (Tom Wolfe's Sherman McCoy or Martin Amis's John Self[3] or even nonfiction's Donald and Ivana Trump), or not young at all (Burt Reynolds, Zsa Zsa Gabor, Rupert Murdoch, Tammy Faye Bakker[4]), they all seem to survive, nay thrive, on a cultural diet whose nutritional equivalent is sugar and preservatives. Though the examples I have provided are either public or fictional figures, they are types for a huge number of modern-day people. They do not ask the bigger questions of life, they simply do not need to. The twentieth century has washed away the solid cultural ground beneath their feet, and they have learned to survive with no foundations. They are not desperate or morally remiss. On the contrary, they are the public, and the more successful of them are greatly admired, the stuff of TV talk shows, gossip columns, and chic magazines.

Fifty years ago, Victor Frankl, in his legendary book *Man's Search for Meaning*,[5] described the world of the mid-twentieth century in categories that remain illuminating in a postmodernity that he did not exactly envisage. He saw Western civilization as existing in a condition of "existential vacuum" that resulted from the destruction of culture. Without culture, individuals are alone to establish standards and decide conduct, and most cannot cope with this. With the will to meaning exhausted they fall victims to boredom and either do what everyone else does or do what someone tells them to do. They select one of two ersatz absolutes, the will to power or the will to pleasure, idolizing either money or sex. Frankl proposed the curative regimen of "being responsible," either to self, society, or God, thus effectively reestablishing the will to meaning and becoming once again a subject rather than a victim of cultural forces.

We would be hard-pressed to find a more acute and economical analysis of late-twentieth-century cultural malaise. Frankl was prescient in his writings, but what he did not foresee was that it is possible to live, apparently happily, within the world of the false absolutes. The cure is not taken because the disease is not recognized. Frankl's insights grew out of his experiences in concentration camps, and he correctly saw the true danger of these places was the destruction of the self, rather than the destruction of the body. In postmodernity, however, many seem able to live without a real identity, worshiping one or both of the two idols. In the haunting words of Dorothee Soelle, the world is like a giant super-market where "absent-mindedly yet at the same time absorbed in what we are doing, we push our shopping-carts up one aisle and down the other, while death and alienation have the run of the place."[6]

For the second type of postmodern human being, modernity *is* the enemy, defined as a mix of liberalism, moral relativism, and "secular humanism." These individuals are at one and the same time postmodern and premodern. Most inhabit our world somewhat comfortably, some make use of its technology and expertise, and they may even share so many of its values and consume so much of its production, yet they also hark back to a premodern world for their basic values, and—most importantly—they seem to see no conflict in this position. Pope John Paul II is a good example of this type, as, in a different way, is Camille Paglia. We could expand the list with Jerry Falwell and Richard John Neuhaus from the world of religious thought, Ronald Reagan or Margaret Thatcher from political life, Pat Robertson from somewhere between the two. There is a range of subtypes here, from the fundamentalists to the neoconservatives to the postliberals, united in their suspicion of the recent past and their attempt at the retrieval of what they perceive to be characteristics of an earlier time—certainty or community or tradition or family.

The third type of postmodern individual is more difficult to categorize. These people know they are postmodern, not so much in the sense that they would recognize or embrace the label as that they consent to their presence in today's world, take it seriously, relish some of it, and challenge other facets. They are critically present in and to their postmodern world. I would hope that most of my readers and I could be included in this category, since the ruling characteristic of critical openness seems to me to be required of any Christian reading of history that takes seriously the reality of grace and the presence of the Spirit. The task of discerning where in the world grace and the Spirit are being poured out is intensely difficult, but the conviction that it is happening is a sine qua non for a hopeful appropriation of our world.

There is a distinctly tentative quality to the above pages, as the reader who has reached this point will surely have noted. But the challenge of discussing postmodernity is not like that of describing a brick or weighing a pound of nails. We are trying, as they say, to hit a moving target, one, moreover, that we the discussants are also aboard. Although the wise philosopher will await the dusk and take on the role of Minerva's owl, the urgency of religious reflection can be allowed no such leeway. Now is the time in which theological reflection takes place, because now is the moment of grace, of salvation, of evangelization. The theological question of Christian presence in the postmodern world cannot be put without an at least provisional and tentative characterization of the one being evangelized, and thus we make our apologia.

Postmodern Thought

Our age is, in especial degree, the age of criticism, and to criticism everything must submit.

—Immanuel Kant

There exists a variety of perspectives within contemporary thought, both more narrowly philosophical discussion and broader cultural criticism, which take seriously the cultural phenomenon of postmodernity discussed previously. Those thinkers who ignore culture and those who dismiss postmodernity as faddish superficiality will not take up our time, though thoughtful critics of postmodernity undoubtedly will. Seriousness about postmodernity, from whatever perspective, is in fact closely linked to a somewhat different issue, namely, attitudes to the Enlightenment project of *modernity*. Postmodern thought, indeed, is a series of attitudes struck in face of questions bequeathed by modernity about the character of rationality, the nature of subjectivity, issues of rights and responsibility, and the constitution of the political community. While the precise delineation of the gamut of postmodern thought can be complex, a basic taxonomy is relatively straightforward. Some thinkers—let us call them, for now, *late moderns*—find the project of modernity unfinished, and wish to carry it forward, albeit in the vastly changed world of cultural postmodernity. Others—the *true postmoderns*—see in the exhaustion of modernity and its unmasking as simply the latest in a long line of totalizing discourses the chance to move forward into a radical historicism. Still others—let us call them the *countermoderns*—celebrate the demise of modernity as an opportunity to return to the securities of an earlier age.

The late modern, postmodern, and countermodern options for confronting the project of modernity can be seen interacting in relation to the latest phases of three issues in post-Enlightenment culture. The first, epistemological, issue centers on the notion of subjectivity. What is a self or a subject, and how does it encounter the world? The second, ethical, issue emerges from considering modern responses to the demise of metaphysical, religious, or other foundational approaches to morality, and finding them inadequate to the ethical pluralism of today. The third, or sociopolitical, issue is often characterized as the question of otherness: when we decenter the subject, the male, the European, how can we move beyond power relations to envisage another way for communities to be present to one another? But before turning to examine these areas of debate, I want to begin by outlining that problem of modernity toward which, in the end, the varieties of postmodern thought evince this range of attitudes.

What Is Enlightenment?

Intellectual debate today over the "problem of modernity" is a matter of assessing the import of what the Western world inherited from the Enlightenment. The Enlightenment gave us the autonomy of human reason, the notion of human rights, and the struggle for a just and equitable society.[7] At the same time, it is largely responsible for the markedly individualistic cast of "developed" Western society and implicated in the anomie and social disintegration that accompanies development. The Enlightenment is the source of the intellectual ferment that resulted in the technological marvels of the late twentieth century. It has also promoted the exercise of instrumental reason, lauded human domination over the natural world, and at least made it more difficult for human beings to draw nourishment from the more communitarian of their impulses. As Theodor Adorno and Max Horkheimer put it in the title of their most influential work, we have to recognize a "dialectic of enlightenment,"[8] and all of today's cultural critics and social philosophers have to make their own assessment of the balance of positive and negative forces within it.

The Enlightenment project of modernity was and remains the triumph of reason and the mastery of the human mind over the external world. But in the course of the two centuries since Immanuel Kant's well-known essay, "What Is Enlightenment?"[9] such a simple delineation of the tasks has come to seem intensely problematic. Opening by quoting the motto adopted in 1736 by the influential Society of the Friends of Truth, Horace's *Sapere aude!* (Dare to know!), Kant argued that the removal of all external constraints from the use of reason is the distinctive mark of the Enlightenment. The authority of both religion and metaphysics is replaced by the individual exercise of critical reason and, as the quotation at the head of this section asserts, there are then no limits to what may be subjected to critique. Two centuries after Kant, however, thinkers in his debt have carried critique to lengths that he did not envisage, while others eschew the notion of critique altogether. There are many who recognize more subtle constraints than those Kant eliminated, and many who deny the reality of the critiquing subject itself.

For Kant, the freedom of the individual from all constraints upon thought means that the subject can become an object to itself, and can thus come to know itself ultimately as a transcendental subject over against the world as a whole. Here for the first time in the history of philosophy, thinks Michel Foucault, the nature of the philosophizing subject is placed under the scrutiny of the same subject's critical reason. Philosophy, in a complete break with the givenness of René Descartes's doubting (but not self-doubting) ego, takes on a self-referential character. But because he believes that Kant has, all unwittingly, also raised the portentous question of the character of the present moment, Foucault can reject Kant's transcendental subject and yet estimate his legacy highly. Kant has formulated "the question of the present as the philosophical event to which the philosopher who speaks of it belongs."[10] When religion and metaphysics are renounced as guides, contingency replaces foundations. As Foucault wrote in his final essay on Kant's "What Is Enlightenment?" the modern human being is not the one "who goes off to discover himself, his secrets and his hidden truth," but rather "the man who tries to invent himself."[11]

For Foucault, then, Kant stands at the beginning of a discourse of modernity that has over time taken two quite different directions, toward an "analytics of truth" and toward an "ontology of the present, an ontology of ourselves." The first direction is the one that would normally be associated with Kant, an investigation of the conditions of possibility of knowledge, and Foucault cannot go along with this supreme exercise in subject-centered reason. Indeed, Foucault's work as a whole can be seen as the destruction of such a philosophical perspective, and those who remain committed to it, he thinks, exhibit a "piety" toward the Enlightenment that "is of course the most touching of treasons." The second direction, toward an "ontology of the present," preserves the Enlightenment legacy in a different sense, namely, it preserves the meaning of the event of the Enlightenment, "the question of the historicity of thinking about the universal."[12] And so Foucault, a philosopher best known for his commitment to the dissolution of the subject, can make the surprising claim that he stands in the Kantian tradition.

Jürgen Habermas, a thinker normally at odds with Foucault, expresses an essentially similar estimation of Kant's essay,[13] also finding two distinct paths that stem ultimately from the Enlightenment legacy, but describing and valuing them differently. Habermas recognizes the Kantian destruction of the unified premodern world of myth, metaphysics, and religion, and its replacement by the transcendental subject whose powers of reason organize experience. Thus, the premodern authority of metaphysics or religion over the reasoning subject collapses. Metaphysics and religion become instead subdivisions of experience, and thus dimensions of subjectivity. The originary unity is fragmented; the reasoning subject replaces it.

Habermas's next step is to echo G. W. F. Hegel's critique of Kant, namely, that the principle of subjectivity is not itself sufficient to re-create the unifying power of religion: "the modern world . . . posited as absolute something that was conditioned."[14] In other words, in Kant's notion of transcendental subjectivity Hegel finds an attempt on the part of the finite subject to shoulder an infinite task, an attempt doomed to failure.[15] At this fateful moment, thinks Habermas, two paths lie open before Hegel. He can stay with the unifying power of intersubjectivity, laid out in his earliest works, or he can turn to a notion of absolute spirit. That he chooses the latter locks him into the philosophy of subjectivity, and carries modern thought down the wrong track. Kant's error and Hegel's misguided solution to it lead directly to the destruction of rationality and the dissolution of the subject perpetrated by the intellectual descendants of Friedrich Nietzsche. Thus Kant, in specifying Enlightenment in the way he does, inaugurates modernity, but opens it to the depredations of postmodern thought.

While Foucault and Habermas both value Kant as the initiator of the discourse of modernity, the different directions in which they interpret subsequent developments indicate the two main paths that contemporary thought takes in the face of the Enlightenment. For Foucault, Jacques Derrida, Georges Bataille, and others, subjectivity is a chimera and the project of modernity is accordingly exhausted. For Habermas, Charles Taylor, and others of a more moderate persuasion, the bankruptcy of the notion of a transcendental subject does not mean the end of subjectivity. Instead, a dialogically or politically engaged reason and a situated subjectivity must be asserted for philosophical discourse to be recognized as the latest phase in the Enlightenment project.[16] There is, of course, a third position, which is the rejection of modernity in favor of an option that may at times seem postmodern, and which is in many respects comfortable with certain aspects of postmodern culture. This premodern or even countermodern stance is happy with a world in which reason is not so much inscribed in the subject, but rather found in the subject's sharing in and reflecting a rationality that transcends it, and whose highest expression is something like the divine self-thinking thought of Greek metaphysics.

It is now possible to be more precise about three distinct attitudes to the postmodern world. The first and most clearly postmodern is the radical historicist perspective, most frequently associated with the work of Foucault and poststructuralism in general (though Foucault himself never accepted the poststructuralist designation), but also possessing influential variations in the writings of Derrida, Richard Rorty, and the neopragmatist camp,[17] and the whole movement of French feminist writing represented by Julia Kristeva and Luce Irigaray. While it is possibly rash to attempt generalizations about these radical historicists, and while there are many differences and disputes between them, three things at least can be said that seem to be true of all of them. First, they all in their different ways reject any theory of knowledge that involves placing the traditional notion of the subject at the center. Second, they would all agree that "reason" is a contextual and relative reality, rather than an absolute or transcendental one. And third, each would find that the examination of this reason reveals its dependence on something else, perhaps on power relations or desire. Here, genealogy often replaces critique, aesthetics takes over from ethics, irony triumphs, and political engagement cannot be easily justified. It may be grasped in ways that would seem counterintuitive, or it may be a kind of guerrilla warfare against "the 'micro-fascism' of everyday life."[18]

At the other extreme of postmodern thought we encounter an attitude (again, not a school or group) that I wish to call the postmodernism of nostalgia. Individuals as various as Martin Heidegger, Allan Bloom, and Theodor Adorno can be found sheltering under this particular umbrella, although it is likely they would be facing away from one another! In Heidegger's thought the human individual is a "region" or "clearing" in which Being may appear, and the being which may appear is definitely the Being of Greek metaphysics rather than the debased conception exhibited in Western philosophy's "forgetfulness of Being." Conservative cultural critics like Allan Bloom and Daniel Bell in their different ways find modernism to be a Gadarene slide from the assertion of the autonomous reasoning subject to the libidinous narcissism of the leftist intellectual. They either hark back like Bloom to a more classical age, or celebrate—like Bell—a new class of technocrats whose discipline and efficiency usher in the austere plenty of a new economic order, but whose personal tastes and conventional values belong to a premodern world. Habermas comments drily on the neoconservative distaste for philosophical modernism: "Intellectuals undermine the authority of strong institutions and simple traditions."[19]

Between the two attitudes, there is a third to be encountered, no less amorphous than the historicist and the nostalgic. Under the rubric of "late modernism" I want to include thinkers who choose to remain consciously in the tradition of reason and subjectivity, but who nevertheless recognize that post-Enlightenment developments have enormously complicated the question of what the subject is and how, if at all, notions of universal reason can still be maintained. They form no school but can be associated together rather, as Foucault said of modernity in general, because they demonstrate an attitude, that of a commitment to the unfinished character of the project of modernity in a distinctly postmodern world, though with varying degrees of closeness to the Enlightenment and distance from radical postmodernism. Three quite distinct and occasionally opposed directions within this group can be identified: Jürgen Habermas's assertion of communicative reason and commitment to a discourse ethic;[20] Charles Taylor's endorsement of the attempt to develop "anthropologies of situated freedom," to overcome the polarization between advocates of "self-responsible reason and freedom on the one hand," and those on the other who feel that to counter this they must be proponents of a "disengaged subjectivity";[21] and Jean-François Lyotard's assertion of postmodernism as but a moment within modernism itself.

The three fundamental attitudes to the project of modernity that I have outlined above—radical postmodern, nostalgic postmodern or countermodern, and late modern—will be woven in and out within the remaining pages of this chapter, as we consider postmodern thought's attempt to deal with three bequests from modernity: the disappearance of the subject, ethical relativism, and the character of otherness.

The Problem of Subjectivity

While it is true that from at least the time of the Sophists onwards, philosophers have asked whether we can know anything with certainty, and in more modern times have debated whether knowledge is a matter of the perception of external reality or the organizing power of the human mind, few thinkers before the relatively recent past ever questioned the integrity of the knowing subject itself. Late-eighteenth-century critics of the Enlightenment either challenged its prideful vision of the ultimate triumph of human reason in the fulfillment of human power and achievement (like Joseph de Maistre or Edmund Burke) or (like Johann Gottfried Herder and Giambattista Vico) championed a view of the autonomy and incommensurability of different societies, and hence denied the possibility of universally applicable objective values. But not even this second group could justifiably be called relativist, or was ever even close to recognizing what Isaiah Berlin calls "the mazes of false consciousness."[22]

Before the nineteenth-century implosion of self-consciousness, two basic kinds of attitudes to the human subject and its powers can be discerned. Either the human being is understood in terms of something larger, or is the seat of reason and the originator of meaning. On the one hand, there is the humble certitude of the essentially religious self, on the other the self-confident aggression of the Enlightenment human being. The one is aware that the human being is small, limited, and sinful, but places its trust in the creator God who is the fullness of all perfections, including that of reason (or, in a secular analogue, understands the human world in function of some overarching metaphysical reality). The other is equally convinced of the capacity of universal reason, in which all human beings share, in principle to comprehend all that is and to usher in a utopian society. In neither case (nor, as we have noted, among more historicist critics of the Enlightenment) is any doubt cast upon the subject's capacity to grasp an external objective reality, and still less is there any doubt about the subject/object distinction itself.

The potential for analysis of the human subject in truly tragic terms is only awakened in the nineteenth century, with notions of the Romantic hero on the one hand, and the dissolution of selfhood in the great "masters of suspicion" (Karl Marx, Nietzsche, and Sigmund Freud) on the other. Either the human individual is enmeshed in a world that is of its nature not open to final comprehension, or, more radically, the subject is under attack as the product of economic forces, the arena of power, or the interplay of psychic processes. The Cartesian ego gives way to the Freudian ego and the seeds of the postmodern attitude are sown long before the postmodern world becomes a reality.

By the late nineteenth century the philosophy of consciousness was in retreat, and although Husserlian phenomenology represents a kind of last-ditch attempt to reassert it, all other great philosophical voices of the twentieth century have made, in their different ways, what has come to be called "the linguistic turn."[23] It is not Being or God or *nous* or reason that is the foundation of thinking, and hence of the subject, but language. What can be said lays down the boundaries of what can be thought, and this insight has profound historicizing and contextualizing implications. Any and every linguistic formulation bears the marks of the culture and history out of which it has emerged, and there can then be no such thing as a universal language—nor therefore a universal reason—as a tool for the comprehension of reality, standing outside that historical reality. Rhetoric, mathematics, physics, and the arts come together in the assertion that, because the observer is always already a part of the world of that which is observed, knowledge cannot be pure, may not even aspire to the condition of purity. Language is not, as Heidegger would have it, the "house of Being," but simultaneously its creator and destroyer.

It would be an error, however, to imagine that philosophical thought and cultural criticism "after modernity" are homogeneous phenomena. While no one can escape the judgment that the "linguistic turn" has occurred, a range of reactions to this fact can be detected, varying from regret at the false step, to excitement at the challenge this represents, to disappointment that it has not been recognized for the closet foundationalism that rigorous consideration will reveal it to be. Heideggerian metaphysical nostalgia, Habermasian reconstructionist modernity, and the radical historicism of Foucault are all attempts to think beyond the philosophy of subjectivity.

The practitioners of radical postmodern thought see in the Enlightenment's strong notion of subjectivity the seeds of social and political repression. Thus, their own project of the destruction of subjectivity is linked directly to the ideal of human emancipation. To them, modernity is viewed as a gigantic conspiracy, which their work exists to unmask. The assertion of the transcendental subject, "mastering" (a telling word in this context) the universe, privileges the powerful, the European, the male—the skilled manipulators of the social, economic, and political system. In the name of freedom, modernity has in fact radically curtailed freedom, substituting not so much a police state as a series of ideologies which, freely embraced, enchain individuals in ways at once the most sophisticated and most difficult to throw off. The way forward is then to unmask the illusion of subjectivity.

This general point can be illustrated in the work of Foucault, in many ways the most influential of this group of thinkers. Foucault's social focus is upon what he calls the "normalization" process in society, by which he means the multifarious ways in which society becomes organized on a "rational" basis, and even how societies become homogenized internally and in relation to one another. Since his work is by his own declaration a form of "genealogy," he must proceed from close consideration of historical events, an approach at its clearest in his discussion of the penal system, *Discipline and Punish*.[24] But this work is also very instructive about the complexities of his project. It tells the story of the transformation of punishment and the growth of the prison, from the obvious and almost unbearable cruelties heaped upon "Damien the regicide" in the famous opening pages of the book, to the apparently relatively humane phenomena of incarceration and rehabilitation that emerged first in the earlier part of the nineteenth century. It is also, according to Foucault, to be read as an allegory about "the soul" which is "effect and instrument of political anatomy" and the "prison of the body."[25] In this book Foucault gives clearest expression to his view that knowledge and power are inseparable from one another, and indeed that knowledge is achieved through the exercise of power (whether used productively or negatively). Thus the very notion of a "reason" unimplicated in the power/knowledge nexus is denied, just as the persistent invocation of this ideal is itself revealed as a device of the normalizing state to constrain the individual while preserving the appearance of emancipation. The Enlightenment, concludes Foucault, "which discovered the liberties, also invented the disciplines."[26] Moreover, in the general exercise of "supervision," of which penal discipline is only the most evident and most extreme form, society inscribes the "soul" upon the body, and by so doing subjects the individual to the coercions of "psyche, subjectivity, personality, consciousness . . . and the moral claims of humanism."[27] It is from this prison that the postmodern human being must struggle to emerge.

If the genealogy is elaborated in works like *Discipline and Punish*, the "ontology of ourselves" which it implies is to be found above all in *The Order of Things*.[28] Here, Foucault outlines his theory of "doubling," in which he indicates as clearly as ever he did the ambiguities in the traditional notion of the subject. When, in the language of the project of modernity, I say "I," three "doubles" are invoked. First, "I" am the one who constitutes the object world for me as a subject, but I am also an object within that world. Second, I am aware of myself as a product of forces that I cannot know (and thus I am a self freed from the captivity of not knowing I am such a product), yet I remain a product of these unknown forces, and so I am to that degree not free. Third, I am the moment from which history unfolds, the past, present, and future viewed in relation to me, but I also have a history that antedates me and that I cannot control. The modern project, thinks Foucault, is to have the subjective poles triumph over the objective, but that leads only to a spurious certainty and the encouragement of impulses to control and domination. This direction must be rejected in favor of a search for a self beyond humanism, beyond this doubling and so beyond the privileging of a dominating, subjective self, over an objective reality.

The contrast between the radical historicist position vis-à-vis the project of modernity and that of the "late moderns" is nicely captured by Richard Rorty when he writes: "Michel Foucault is an ironist who refuses to be a liberal, whereas Jürgen Habermas is a liberal who is unwilling to be an ironist."[29] The ironist is the one who is willing to live with the ambiguity encountered, for example, in the multiple "doubling" of the self. The nonironist must resolve the ambiguity, and this Habermas does through invoking the paradigm of intersubjectivity.

Like Foucault, Habermas wants to pass beyond the instrumentalization of reality that takes place when my starting point is that I am a subject and everything else is for me an object. On the contrary, says Habermas, I am constituted as a self in my intersubjective communicative praxis. Habermas's linguistic turn, like that of so many twentieth-century philosophers, carries him away from the philosophy of consciousness to the philosophy of language. But for Habermas there is a difference. The linguistic unit upon which the philosopher must concentrate, and that forms whatever foundation there is to human subjectivity, is *the speech act.* The act of communication rests upon certain fundamental characteristics and so is in a sense foundational, but the foundation is only formal, not substantive. Thus, intersubjective communication can only occur because there is an assumption on both parts that the speaker is comprehensible, sincere, truthful, and exhibits recognizable ethical norms. Deceit, lying, manipulation are possible only because the speaker can take advantage of the hearer's assumption that the rules of discourse are operative.

For Habermas, then, while an individual may utilize instrumental reason to manipulate a whole arsenal of technology and day-to-day mechanical operations, the individual is constituted as a subject, that is, in dealings with other individuals, not through the essentially instrumental relation that would be operative in a subject/object paradigm, but intersubjectively in the praxis of communicative reason. Moreover, this "communicative action" not only demonstrates formal foundational structures, but also requires an openness toward the other, manifested both in a commitment to the equal participation of all in the discourse and to an ongoing intersubjective process oriented to arriving at norms for action. The community of intersubjective communicative action is thus revealed to be both emancipatory and committed to a consensus theory of truth.

If communicative action is the distinctive process by which human sociality should be governed, its efficacy and even effective existence is under threat. The problem for Habermas is that today's postmodern world illustrates the virtual triumph of instrumental over communicative reason. To use for once his own sometimes exotic formulations, the system has "colonized" the life-world. The model of communicative action has been almost squeezed out of all but the purely private, domestic realm by that of instrumental reason. This is the truth behind the common complaints heard today about the decline of community and the rise of public violence. People, the critics are saying, are too busy using others like machines rather than engaging them as equal selves in the intersubjective process of communicative action.

The "postmodern" world for Habermas is a product of an unbalanced development of the Enlightenment legacy. The radical individualism that is concomitant upon the assertion of the primacy of the reasoning subject and its potential mastery over an objective world of things erodes the *community* of freedom. Thus, the modern community of selves is left naked and exposed, prey to an instrumental order—the social apparatus—now reified as the system to which the human impulse must increasingly bow. Moreover, the systemic drive of modern society now reinforces the individualism out of which it grew, in order further to entrench itself as "the way things must be." This is the connection, in Habermas's mind, between postmodern society and neoconservatism. From subjectivity, the path leads smoothly to ethics and politics.

Nostalgic postmodernism has its philosophical giant in the overwhelming presence of Martin Heidegger in twentieth-century thought. Heidegger is well known for accusing the Western world of having abandoned metaphysics and so ended up in the alienated condition of "everydayness." What is perhaps not so often noted is that the proposals he makes for overcoming our plight are couched almost entirely in the language of looking back, of return, of recovery, in a word, of "nostalgia."[30] In our moment of crisis, we must overcome our "forgetfulness of Being," but the Being to be recovered is both of mythic proportions and of mythic quality. It is one of those "big" ideas that Rorty has perceptively observed are so dear to the great modern philosophers. And it is shrouded in something, whether the veils of antiquity, mystery itself, or the obfuscatory prose style of Heidegger. It is a big, fuzzy idea, but it serves its purpose, which is to lay upon the Western philosophical tradition and the everyday world of twentieth-century Europe the charge of plain bad faith.

Heidegger's nostalgia is further demonstrated in his attention to subjectivity. In his essay, "What Is Metaphysics?"[31] Heidegger writes of human being (*Dasein*) as "being projected into Nothing," so that it can thereby confront "the totality of what-is," and "this 'being beyond' what-is we call transcendence."[32] If human being did not stand outside the totality of what-is, it could not relate to it, and so could not relate to itself. Now this is certainly not the Kantian transcendental subject, for Heidegger's *Dasein* is only the "clearing" in which Being manifests itself, and so is itself instrumental to some higher metaphysical reality. The subject is neither the human nor the "I," but a kind of substrate or foundation. Only with Descartes does the notion of subject become restricted to the "relational center of that which is as such."[33] As a result of which, of course, everything else becomes an object to the subject, and the problem of modern science and technology is born. Domination becomes the human way of being in the world. The woodland path (*Holzweg*) from subjectivity to ethics and politics is neither long nor overgrown.

Even in this short discussion, the variations among thinkers confronting postmodernity are clear. The radical view rejects the transcendental subject in favor of utter contingency, true to its roots in Nietzsche's project. The late modern approach continues to attend to the idea of the subject, but finds it differently constituted. The nostalgic form of postmodernity harks back to an essentially religious view in which the subject is there, but understood in terms of something larger than its own petty subjectivity. For reasons of space, only one major thinker has been invoked thus far in each category. But as we turn now to ethical and then to sociopolitical issues of postmodernity, others who evince the characteristics of the same attitudes will be drawn into the conversation.

The Problem of Relativism

The ethical issue of postmodernity is relatively easy to describe, though finding a satisfactory resolution is a much greater challenge. The dissolution of metaphysics and religion in the Enlightenment as foundations of a settled universe led not only to the demise of premodern subjectivity and the appearance of the transcendental subject of modernity, but also to the disappearance of moral authority based on religious and metaphysical values, and their replacement by a finite subject imposing its own moral vision upon the world. But while Enlightenment moral reasoning rebuffed the appeals to authority in scripture and the monarch's will, its claims were no less universal. External authority is simply replaced by an equally demanding internal voice. The Kantian categorical imperative—so act that the maxim by which you act, you could will to be a universal law—implies universally applicable categories of right and wrong. And it places an enormous burden upon the practitioner of pure practical reason. To return to Hegel's criticism, the finite subject is being asked to shoulder an infinite task.

Two hundred years after Kant, the ethical map looks very different. Postmodern thought is as unhappy with an unadulterated transcendental judgment as it is with the invocation of religious authority or ethical absolutes. The freedom of the subject championed by Kant has stretched way beyond the bounds he envisaged, and the questions are now different. What is the relationship between the ethical judgments of different individuals, and what are the implications of different ethical languages? Are there any truth judgments to be made at all anymore, or is it all a matter of "warranted assertability"?[34] How do we adjudicate between the competing claims of ethical relativism, ethical pluralism, and ethical subjectivism? And is the very language of ethics not simply another discourse whose result, if not its objective, is to impose upon rather than enable human freedom?

Contemporary moralists display a range of responses to these and related issues not dissimilar from the spectrum of opinions on the postmodern threat to subjectivity. At one extreme, radical postmodern thinkers have simply replaced ethics with either aesthetics or irony. Rather than understand decision making as a process of conforming to or articulating truth, some see it to be a matter of crafting a life or inventing a self.[35] An ironist like Richard Rorty wants to maintain the right to such a private self-creation alongside a social concern "to make our institutions and practices more just and less cruel"[36] without trying to achieve some theoretical reconciliation of these two impulses. From a much less liberal perspective, Foucault attempted a similarly theoretically unjustifiable political engagement. At the other extreme are those thinkers who recognize this trend in postmodern ethics and see it as a direct consequence of the impossibility of Enlightenment ethics (a finite subject shouldering an infinite task). In response, these conservatives embrace a myth of decline and fall in calling for a return either to an authoritarian religious ethics, or, in more sophisticated manner, to an Aristotelian ethic of virtue.[37] Between the two can be found a number of responses that seek to keep some version of the ethical project of modernity alive in a philosophical world beyond foundations—perhaps through some weak or procedural foundationalism (like the "discourse" ethics of Habermas[38]), or some "moderate pragmatism" that holds out for a notion of truth while admitting a plurality of moral perspectives.[39]

At the center of ethical concerns today, in the academy and—more importantly—in daily life, is the issue of moral relativism. While this term can be understood, and is sometimes used, to mean that "anything goes" in ethics, and that anyone's point of view is as good as any other, or just as good for that person as mine is for me, this is not where the real issue lies. Rather, we have to ask what is the *relation* between the moral judgments of different individuals, or even what is the *relation* between different conceptions of the notion of moral authority itself. The academic debate is fueled by suspicion of any notion of universal reason and the recognition of the cultural relativity and historicity of concepts and categories of understanding. The everyday problem is closer to home. It is not so much a matter of discerning whether and why cannibalism is appropriate to some and "abominable" (Jeffrey Stout's term) for others, but how I can talk to my neighbor, colleague, or fellow citizen about what is right or true or good, absent an authority to which to refer our respective judgments.

Jeffrey Stout, not unlike most thinkers influenced to a degree by neopragmatism, points to the importance of utilizing everyday practices to shed light on the philosophical issues. What is instructive about my debate with my neighbor, even if this person shares little or no common cultural or religious background with me, is that we proceed for the most part on the assumption that there are some things we have in common, and that there are some human constants—otherwise, presumably, we could not converse at all. This "language of perspicuous contrasts" (Charles Taylor's phrase) enables us to talk, uncovering areas of agreement and areas where we must agree to differ. Moral relativism, in other words, is only possible on the basis of some degree of mutual understanding. As the dialogue proceeds, what we must hope for is "overlapping consensus,"[40] not perfect concord on the nature of the good. This seemingly relaxed and even casual attitude of "modest pragmatism" is actually built upon a commitment to some hard realities. There are no fundamental principles to be determined, the argument goes, even in the Judeo-Christian ethic, though there are of course truths fundamental to this or that tradition and there is nothing wrong with a personal commitment to these truths. There is no comfort to be found in some metaphysic or religious vision or epistemological certitude, but judgments on what is true or justifiable must still be made. There is no path to utopia (or, as Jeffrey Stout puts it, "When you unwrap the utopia, the batteries aren't included"), but the responsibility to seek to render the world "better" or "less cruel" persists. There may be no common human nature or human reality, but the demands of sociality continue. Isolation in self-creation is logically impossible and—dare I say it?—morally opprobrious.

The aesthetic wing of postmodern thought denies the dimension of social responsibility, and ethics becomes solely a matter of self-invention. In its profound individualism, curiously enough, it stands in that Kantian tradition it professes to despise. For example, David R. Hiley has written perceptively of the extent to which Foucault's ethics remain linked to the Kantian orientation to autonomy. But, attempting to rescue Foucault from Habermas's accusation of neoconservatism and Taylor's charge that there are no resources within Foucault's views for a critique of the present moment, he must cast this autonomy in terms of freedom in relation to normalizing power. So while he is correct to insist that Foucault's "ethics" are not merely naked self-valorization, and do involve an element of "enabling us to be lawgivers for ourselves" (another curious echo of existentialism, though without the guilt), this remains in the end at the service of aesthetics.[41] On the other hand, Foucault's pursuit of Charles Baudelaire's "dandysme" (discussed in Kant's "What Is Enlightenment?" essay) is not simple self-indulgence, requiring the discipline or ascesis (Foucault's term) of any creative activity. But in the final analysis it is the discipline of self-invention, of transgressing those limits that Kant's project existed to define and remain within.[42] Of course, Foucault is in the end only remaining faithful to Kant's observation at the head of this section, that "critique" knows no limits, if carrying it considerably further than Kant himself envisaged.

The claim that critique knows no limits is a particularly vibrant red flag to the traditionalist bull. Conservative social, political, and religious movements worldwide (Christian, Jewish, and Islamic) react to what they see as the socially corrosive effects of the unlimited autonomy championed, in their opinion, by "liberalism." While these large groups, and even their leaders, are unlikely to diagnose the illness in the language of philosophy, what they perceive is in fact what conservative philosophers would identify as the social degeneration consequent upon the impossibility of the Enlightenment project. The conservative public itself is more likely to describe the situation in terms of the failure of "secular humanism" and the consequent need to return to "family values," usually buttressed by the sanctions and rewards of a religious tradition. Either way the concern is to locate the values believed to have been abandoned in favor of some version of moral relativism, though we should note at least two possible ways of articulating the basis for such values. They might, on the one hand, be perceived within some metaphysical scheme of universal reason; they might equally well, on the other, be seen as the values internal to a religious or even a cultural tradition's particular way of viewing the world. They might be rationalist or fideist or, in a more contemporary parlance, they might be either foundationally or nonfoundationally appropriated.[43]

Alasdair MacIntyre's crusade to promote Aristotelian "virtue ethics" is at one and the same time a critique of ethical conservatism and a challenge to the ethical confusion he perceives to exist in postmodernity.[44] On the former count, MacIntyre rejects notions of an ideal human nature that would justify the teleological drive of ethics as the means by which untutored (or "fallen") human nature could approximate its "true" self. On the latter, he castigates the individualism of the contemporary moral and cultural scene. To MacIntyre, Nietzsche's rejection of Enlightenment morality was entirely appropriate, though it has led to the primacy of moral "emotivism" today. But Nietzsche would not have been necessary, had the Enlightenment itself not made the initial mistake of a rejection of Aristotelian ethics of virtue. What we have today, thinks MacIntyre, is an ethics of rules in which those qualities are accounted virtues that advance the functioning of the moral rules. How much more satisfactory was the Aristotelian scheme in which the virtues are prior, and the rules follow.

MacIntyre offers an account of virtues as qualities whose significance is revealed in their relationship to social practices. "Practices," for MacIntyre, are cooperative activities possessed of realizable internal goods; virtues are qualities that enable the realization of these goods. Practices, to be practices, must offer complex satisfactions to those who engage in them. MacIntyre suggests that tic-tac-toe is not a practice, chess is. Growing turnips is not a practice, farming is. The general idea is easy to grasp, even if we might disagree about growing turnips (or, say, orchids) though probably not about tic-tac-toe. The internal goods are the particular delights and satisfactions of chess or farming, whereas the money or fame to be accumulated through the expert performance of either are external goods. And the virtues are those qualities—courage, prudence, and so on—that make possible the achievement of the internal goods peculiar to the particular social practice.[45]

The import of all this is that virtues do not just enable us to achieve the internal goods, but also motivate us in the search for the good. Virtues are utilized in the search for the good; therefore a life spent practicing the virtues is a good life. And furthermore, says MacIntyre, it is impossible to conceive of such a life from the standpoint of modern individualism. The search is always begun from and conducted within a particular social identity, even though I may overleap the constraints of that community. Finally, though this reference to community and hence to tradition may sound conservative, it is not, since a healthy tradition "is always partially constituted by an argument about the goods the pursuit of which gives to that tradition its particular point and purpose."[46] This final point may be a little disingenuous on MacIntyre's part. True, such a "healthy" tradition will consequently contain within it a self-critical component. But it is also clear that such self-criticism might well seek to restore supposedly lost goods. Indeed, it is notable that MacIntyre's formulation envisages a purifying evaluation of the goods, but not of the tradition itself.

Focus on the question of moral relativism is, in postmodern hands, a matter of examining the relation between the private and the public self. In their very different ways, both Foucault and Rorty want to be able to deny any theoretical connection between the self-creation of the individual and social responsibility, but both choose to engage with the world socially and even politically. The late moderns cannot abide the sense of theoretical separation of private and public because, as they see it, what is implied in their understanding of a self (the issue of subjectivity returns) spills over into public space. And premodern or countermodern thinkers, whether religious conservatives or the virtue ethicists, are equally committed to a link between private and public, however differently they may articulate that relationship. The third and final issue to be considered in this section of the chapter requires an examination of the question of the "public sphere."

The Problem of Otherness

Thus far, we have looked at a range of attitudes to the demise of modernity's autonomous, rational subject, and progressed to consider what options exist for rethinking morality in light of the decentering of the subject. In both cases we identified the late modern attempt to rescue the essence of the project of modernity while recognizing the changed circumstances in which it must be brought to completion. In both, we also saw two quite different celebrations of the end of modernity. The first, which we called radical postmodernism, looked for a brave new world beyond subjectivity and heteronomous morality. The second, the postmodernism of nostalgia, looked back to a golden age of religious or metaphysical authority in which the individual subject was both more secure and less important than the Enlightenment had made her.

We turn now to the political question of postmodernity, here employing the word *politics* in the Aristotelian sense. The postmodern world is not only a world in which we have become intensely aware of other and different cultures, religions, and political and ethnic traditions. It is also a world in which in many places, above all in the United States, these pluriform understandings of reality have come to coexist within the same civic community. What are the opportunities and options, in such a world and within such a society, for the maintenance and nurturing of a tolerant, purposeful, humane, and ethical national or world community?

In the language and categories current in postmodern thought, the political question is most usually addressed in terms of the problem of "otherness." Attention to the phenomenon of foundational binary oppositions in Western thought is a constant among postmoderns. Utilization of such oppositions always takes the form of privileging one term over the other. The other is the Other. So, for example, Thomas Hobbes distinguished between reason and linguistic clarity on the one hand, and unreason, coupled with ambiguous or metaphorical use of language, on the other.[47] The implication is that the former is the basis of secure political life, the latter a recipe for chaos. It is this second, unprivileged, and suspicious dimension that Derrida in particular and poststructuralists in general have come to call the "Other."[48] The Other, then, is the suspect, the deviant, the path not taken, the darkness, the chaos, standing over against the surety and clarity of the subject's chosen practice. It is the female to the male, the black to the white, the East to the West, the native culture to the representative of the Raj, the homosexual to the heterosexual.

It is not that the postmodern world has recognized the existence of the Other, still less that it has deconstructed the illusion of superiority in the assertion that the subjective pole of any binary opposition (me, not the Other) is the seat of reason, but it is a fact that postmodern society is distinguished as never before by the proximity of the Other. Moreover, this nearness is in the form of a problem to be addressed, a reality to which it is necessary to take an attitude. To give a simple example, a century ago the privileged citizens of any developed Western nation, and that of course meant a white male, and probably a Protestant, did not have to confront the Other. One pole of the binary opposition was triumphant. Women, slaves, native peoples, and homosexuals were of course not invisible, but were successfully deproblematized, incorporated into a monological schema of untroubled serenity. So, while they were undoubtedly "others," their status as "Other" was unrecognized.

The unproblematic nature of otherness in earlier times was a result of the prevalence of what Jean-François Lyotard calls "metanarratives."[49] Consciously adopted or unconsciously reflected, metanarratives shape a view of the world. A metanarrative of the triumph of the autonomous individual's reason and its subjection of a wholly instrumental reality drives much of Enlightenment thought. A metanarrative of the heroic individual's life of feeling and strength of will powers the Romantic reaction to Enlightenment thought. The Hegelian metanarrative of Absolute Spirit tries to extract the best from both. Metanarratives of God, of the Great Spirit, of Nature and of human nature, of capitalist achievement and Marxist hope have crisscrossed history and, for Lyotard, lie now like so many broken shards of pottery in the trashcan of the late twentieth century. Possessed of a metanarrative, any one at all, everything is accounted for in a supreme exercise of the comprehension of reality, a tour de force of imagination and a textbook exercise of power in which the Other is only perceived in and through the metanarrative. The power of the narrative renders powerless that which is accounted for. The voice of the Other is unheard, the presence of the Other, as Other, unnoticed. In postmodernity, for Lyotard and many others, the abandonment of metanarrative means the encounter with the Other.

Whether Lyotard's "incredulity toward metanarratives" is an adequate description of postmodernity is not the issue here. More importantly for us, it draws attention to the indubitable importance of the category of "the Other" for an understanding of postmodernity. Moreover, it represents an important strain of what Hal Foster has called "the postmodernism of resistance," which "seeks to deconstruct modernism and resist the status quo."[50] But how easily can it be related to the other two types of response to postmodernity we have previously identified in this chapter? Radical postmodernism's freeing of the Other is readily discernible in the rejection of metanarratives. But how does late modernism deal with metanarrative's new fragility and what is the reaction of nostalgic postmodernism?[51]

Stephen White presents a very cogent explanation of the debates between the late moderns and the radical postmodernists, in terms of the respective weight each gives to a particular form of responsibility and an attendant understanding of language. There are two significant senses of responsibility, says White. There is the responsibility to act, and the responsibility to otherness. The former—quintessentially represented by Habermas—naturally stresses the "action-coordinating" function of language and sees other uses of language as secondary. The latter—the poststructuralists above all—privilege the "world-disclosing" function of language. So for Habermas the world-disclosing function of language must be confirmed through learning processes in which the action-coordinating function of language is dominant, whereas for Derrida Habermas's construction, like all the others, is just another fiction in a thoroughly fictive language. In the language of otherness, a late modern vision like that of Habermas will attempt to account for otherness within the schema—though it will attend to the problematic character of otherness, the integrity of the other's vision, and the sorry history of the forgetfulness of the Other—while a radical vision will insist that however thorough, comprehensive, and sensitive we might be, there is always a surplus of otherness out there that we cannot comprehend, but must encounter and allow to be.

The political implications of the otherness debate are quite dramatic. The radicals are apt to mire themselves in a "perpetual withholding gesture" (White's phrase), that is, in a critical posture out of which a project or plan of action for the amelioration of this or that state of affairs simply never emerges. This tendency to political inertia has frequently been noticed, of course, especially in the case of Derrida, just as it has also often been said that indifference toward political stands or platforms can make this or that thinker a little too willing to fall in with the status quo (one thinks here of Heidegger or Paul de Man). On the other hand, the late moderns are so committed to a totalizing explanation that their "responsibility to otherness" is endangered. The former may be co-opted into the service of a neoconservative paradise in which government is small, real political choice is limited, and state planning is subordinated to playing the market. But the late moderns' action-orientation makes them susceptible to too homogeneous a vision of society. If otherness is forgotten, then the need to allow for a multivalent and polysemous community may be overlooked.

To put the difference between the late moderns and the radicals in the context of metanarratives, it is fairly clear that the former wish to retain *some* metanarrative, albeit a highly sophisticated, "weak," or "thin" account, while the radicals want to settle for swapping stories. The late moderns are promodern in their continued attention to metanarrative, postmodern in their willingness to accept its historicity and fragility. There can no longer be the metanarrative of the transcendental subject, mastering external reality and bringing it under the sway of reason. In its place we may find something like Habermas's narrative of the ideal speech situation, an eschatological vision in which the counterfactual ideal speech situation drives the struggle for human emancipation. But, without God and hence without salvation, it becomes real only in the strength of its participants' commitments, and is lived out in the Stoic hope that Sartre calls despair: "we limit ourselves to a reliance upon that which is within our wills, or within the sum of the probabilities which render our action feasible."[52]

. Another variation on the "thin" metanarrative of the late moderns can be found in the work of Charles Taylor, particularly in *Sources of the Self*.[53] In the opening chapter to this most impressive work, Taylor employs the language of "frameworks" of meaning, rather than metanarratives, but the use is identical. In the past, says Taylor, unquestioned frameworks have worked to help individuals define their lives and measure their richness: "the space of fame in the memory and song of the tribe, or the call of God as made clear in revelation, or, to take another example, the hierarchical order of being in the universe."[54] While frameworks have today become problematic in different ways for different people, all share the sense that no one framework can taken for granted as the basis for all. Some continue to hold that their framework is right and everyone else is wrong. Some take the relativist position that this framework is right for "us" but not necessarily for "them." Others adhere tentatively and provisionally but genuinely to some framework, while seeking greater certainty or greater clarity. Taylor, however, is of the view that all need a believable framework, even those who claim to reject such frameworks. The position that all frameworks are "gratuitous inventions," a position which he labels (in ethical parlance) "naturalism," is "deeply confused."[55] These reductionist or utilitarian views are motivated, he thinks, by a laudable determination to overcome the "elitism" of frameworks that privilege "honor" or "fame" or "rational mastery" or the "transformation of the will," and an equally praiseworthy counteraffirmation of "ordinary life." But an attention to ordinary life is not a matter of approving of just anything. Rather, it privileges a particular manner of living ordinary life, a standard by which I can judge my own life. Even the naturalist position, then, utilizes a framework. Thus the chapter title, "Inescapable Frameworks."

While Taylor admits the reality of a multiplicity of frameworks, and is clearly "postmodern" in recognizing the modern commitment to transcendental subjectivity as one such framework, this does not amount to an acceptance of the radical incommensurability of all such frameworks. If we leave aside Taylor's expressed commitment to a religious framework, which is in fact detachable from much of the argument of the book, we can discern in Taylor's work an attempt to preserve the claims of subjectivity against the postmodern dissolution of the self and against any simplistic attempt to restore premodern notions of the self. For Taylor the subject remains central, but it is a fragile and threatened subjectivity, enmeshed in its own historicity and open to failure.[56] Taylor returns to the subject in the light of a critical but appreciative reading of radical postmodernist thinkers. And, while he comes back to metanarrative, it is one chastened by the awareness of the demand "of attention, of careful scrutiny, of respect for what is there." This demand "emanates from the world," not from the subject. In such a metanarrative, the Other is there to be heard.[57]

What, finally, of the relation to metanarrative of the nostalgic postmoderns? Here we need to distinguish, as we have done in earlier sections of the chapter, between the return to theistic metanarratives of salvation history or metaphysical metanarratives of Being, on the one hand, and on the other, the postliberal metanarratives of "a new dark age" espoused by MacIntyre and many others. While these two directions in nostalgic postmodernism are similar, there are significant differences. One is the fundamentalist reassertion of a premodern vision, secure in the conviction that modernity and what has followed is the work of Satan, to be eradicated, or the philosophical conviction that what we face is a "history of the forgetfulness of Being," and that a critical rereading of the history of philosophy will allow us to recover that ancient openness to Being in which lies our true identity. But the other knows that we cannot go back, and that modernity cannot be revoked. Its nostalgia close to heartbreaking, it does the best it can. Intentional communities replace the City of God, and the walls are built higher to keep out the secular world. In some respects, this may not seem all that far from Taylor's position, in its realism about modernity and its proclamation of spirituality. However, in its defensiveness and, it would seem, real *lack* of hope for the world as a whole, it stands far apart from him. For Taylor, modernity is good; for MacIntyre, quite the opposite.

Such strong metanarratives efface the other once again, this time by situating them as those beyond the Pale with whom we need have no congress, and in fact should not, in peril of our own purity. In the religious vision of fundamentalism, the unsaved are a corrupting influence. In the new Dark Ages, there is light, life, and hope only within the mead hall. Outside is darkness, night, and Grendel in his lair. As John Milbank's neo-Augustinianism would have it, "the absolute Christian vision of ontological peace now provides the only alternative to a nihilistic outlook."[58] The other is not so much wicked as ignorant, and the ignorance consists precisely in the degree to which the full measure of Christian ontological peace is lacking. Another metanarrative: another Other bites the dust.

Postmodern Science: A Note

The aim of science is not to open the door to everlasting wisdom, but to set a limit on everlasting error.

—Bertolt Brecht

It would be a great mistake, though one to which academics are especially susceptible, to imagine that the temper of our postmodern times is best explained philosophically. Philosophy does not dictate or direct culture; it mirrors it. Thus, philosophical shifts can be useful indicators in getting a grip on what is happening in the world, but they do not cause to happen whatever it is that we decide is happening. Culture is not best explained philosophically; but philosophy can explain what is happening in culture. Our contemporary world is not the way it is because of the work of Derrida and Foucault and Rorty, any more than the medieval world was the product of Aquinas or Ockham. Once again, Hegel seems to have got it right, with his famous dictum that philosophy comes along at the end of an age to explain it, like the Owl of Minerva, taking wing at the dusk.

Much the same cautionary observation can be made about the influence of scientific understanding upon the world. Indeed, the caution needs to be expressed more strongly, precisely because in the popular imagination science is *the* explanatory mechanism for knowing what's what. In the complex mix of social and historical forces, scientific models of understanding, and philosophical worldviews, we would be hard-pressed to distinguish causes from effects. There is certainly no clear reason why we should assert that the scientific shifts from a Ptolemaic to a Newtonian to an Einsteinian way of looking at the universe were instrumental in forming the classical, modern, and postmodern ways of being in the world.

The quotation from Brecht's *Galileo* at the head of this brief final section of the chapter (a passage also quoted with approval by James Gustafson) expresses a more modest but still significant role for scientific understanding. Science does not tell us what we must think, but it does tell us what we may not think. Stated this baldly, there is still room for dissent, however, since science has been victim of its own hubris on innumerable occasions. No, if science is to be given such an important role in defining the boundaries within which interpretation can legitimately occur, then it must be a moderate and chastened science. The scientific positivism of the nineteenth century and its descendant, the "scientism" of our technological society today, are far too confident of science's predictive and explanatory capacities to be given the crucial role that Brecht envisages.

"Postmodern science," whether reflective or causative, is that model of scientific understanding conformed to our contemporary intellectual and cultural climate. Perhaps a more informative label for it would be post-Newtonian science, thus indicating the clear parallels between postmodern philosophy, with its overturning of Enlightenment rationalism and optimism, and postmodern science, with its replacement of scientific positivism by such distinctly unpositivist lines of approach to reality as relativity theory, the uncertainty principle, quantum mechanics, and chaos theory.[59] The parallels can also be carried one step further. The rejection of "clear and distinct ideas" characteristic of both postmodern philosophy and science is not so much occasioned by a loss of confidence in the disciplines as it is by a new awareness that what is there to be explained is itself not clear and distinct. So, philosophy does not so much abandon the search for truth as discover that there is a multiplicity of perspectives from which to view the same set of data. And science does not relinquish its experimental methodology or its commitment to rational explanation, but precisely through its methods encounters a reality that is fuzzier. Science either espouses a form of indeterminism, or retains its commitment to determinism while recognizing unpredictability in the way these presumably deterministic scientific laws are actually played out.

Unfortunately, contemporary theology has paid too little attention to the shift in perspective in the scientific community. The reasons for this are not hard to uncover. Since the time of the Enlightenment, science and religions have occupied quite distinct realms. Science has until lately pursued modernity's project of conquering nature and bending it to a human purpose while theology, shut out of the world of philosophy and science in which for most of the history of Christianity it had been an important partner, retired into fideism or psychologism. A privatized religion left the public realm to secular science, and this newly emancipated science succumbed to a species of hermeneutical hubris. Religion and the world were unrelated.[60]

Religion can once again fruitfully "eavesdrop" (Sallie McFague's word) upon science, not so much because religion has changed, but because science has. On the one hand, postmodern scientific inquiry is no longer so sure of its hermeneutical superiority as modern science was, and thus does not by definition exclude any and every form of inquiry that fails the postivistic test. On the other, *what* postmodern science uncovers is a world in which mystery is real, not synonymous with mystification. But at the same time the religion that hopes to benefit from this new openness must eschew its own forms of hubris. It must also emerge from its privatistic ghettos and engage the tentative, provisional, open-ended "common creation story" as the persuasive narrative of our times.

2

Religion

Postmodern Thought and Religion

A proof that faith makes of itself, practice is the justifying visibility of a belief.

—Michel de Certeau

Philosophical, cultural, and scientific changes of the magnitude of those we have attended to in chapter 1 cannot but have a profound impact on religious thought and theology on the one hand, and on the life of the churches themselves on the other. In this second chapter we shall look quite closely at three particular sets of issues, and a range of postmodern responses to each: the postmodern "problem of God," the role of the Christian community in the postmodern world, and the implications of the traditional claims of Christian uniqueness in face of postmodernity's attention to otherness. Before we do this, however, it is necessary to say something in general about the place of Christianity in the postmodern world, and to try to identify the types of responses to postmodernity that emerge from various sectors of the Christian community.

To any but the most unreconstructed of biblical literalists, the challenge of contemporary Christian religious thought is to keep alive in the postmodern world a religious vision created in a distinctly premodern cultural context, honed to a level of sophistication and lived out courageously through many centuries of premodernity. Whether the task is thought of primarily as one of reception or of mediation, there is no gainsaying its reality. We may struggle to find contemporary language and symbols in which the gospel message can be expressed (mediation), or we may determine that the community of faith needs to purify its capacity to hear once again the Christian story in its biblical transparency (reception), but we cannot deny that either path constitutes a challenge.

The peculiar difficulty of contemporary religion's task is made only the more complicated by the fact that where postmodernity must now venture, modernity has already trod. The Enlightenment valorization of the subject and the emergence of an autonomous secular realm, while it was to a degree a product of the Reformation, represented an enormous challenge to Christianity. If Christianity was to survive, it could no longer live quite so unreflectively within the myth. The universe was now so much bigger than the human world, the world so much bigger and more varied than earlier ages had imagined, and the Christian religion one among many. More importantly, God became a postulate of practical reason in the subject's drive to order reality, rather than the bedrock of the medieval life-world. The intellectual challenge for modern theology was to reconcile a theocentric faith with an anthropocentric worldview. And in meeting that challenge, it was engaging at that time in precisely the project that now faces religion in the postmodern world.

Modern theology is an umbrella term for a whole range of theological directions that share an attitude—that of a reasonable accommodation to the Enlightenment project. Thus, the systematic intellectual rigor of G. W. F. Hegel and the more affective path of Friedrich Schleiermacher, however different from one another, are united in their commitment to the mediation of religious thought to a secular world. The work of Johann Adam Möhler and the Catholic Tübingen School represent attempts on the part of the Roman tradition to enter into dialogue with modernity. Late nineteenth-century liberal Protestantism— Albrecht Ritschl, Adolf von Harnack, Ernst Troeltsch—carries this dialogue about as far as it can go. A twentieth-century thinker like Rudolf Bultmann seems to some to have emptied out the Christian baby with the biblical bathwater, and there is no doubt that he carries his demythologization project to an extreme of anthropocentrism never reached, before or after, in Christian theology. Finally, Paul Tillich's "method of correlation" is a transparent—some would say "shameless"—equation of religious and secular wisdom. On the Catholic side, while Pope Pius X's condemnation of modernism in the encyclical letter *Pascendi* reduced, or at any rate delayed, parallel developments, the

French "nouvelle théologie" school of the 1940s and 1950s and, above all, the work of Karl Rahner, represent important initiatives in mediating theology. The zenith (or nadir, depending on your point of view) within the Roman tradition must be accounted the 1965 document of the Second Vatican Council, the Pastoral Constitution on the Church in the Modern World (*Gaudium et Spes*) with its rejection of the church/world dichotomy and its breathtaking recognition that the church, indeed, can learn from the world.

The "attitude" of modern theology is shared, then, by an assortment of theological outlooks. While many would frequently be antithetical to one another, they all to a greater or lesser degree reflect several assumptions about the theological task. In the first instance, they are all committed to taking seriously the historicality of the biblical texts. Historical-critical method is employed as a matter of course. All recognize the important role of human agency in revelation, including the elements of imagination and creativity.[1] All are deeply suspicious of any exclusivist understanding of Christian salvation. And all, undoubtedly, can be classified as mediating theologies. To put it slightly differently, all would, in some synchronous theological world, come under the scrutiny of Karl Barth, and all would be found wanting.

Theologies in postmodernity try to find their way between two familiar extremes. At one end lies the liberal dissolution of the specificity of Christianity and a thorough accommodation to the world, often masked by a turn to the pietistic or the emotional that in the end cedes the realm of intellect to secular wisdom. At the other end lie fideisms, both biblical and ecclesial. But the world between the two extremes is anything but familiar, a strange landscape of poststructuralists, deconstructionists, chaos theorists, and entropy junkies, struggling for conceptual or metaphorical control over a bewilderingly complex world and a stunningly vast profusion of data. The theologies that emerge from this task bear the marks more of temperament than ideology: there are the timid, the devil-may-care, and the pragmatic, and this in itself is enough to label all of them "postmodern."

Theological responses to the demise of modernity break down into three groups that parallel the three trajectories of postmodern philosophical thought we examined in chapter 1. Some attempt to continue the modern theological project into the postmodern world: for them, postmodern theology is late modern theology. Others see modern theology in irretrievable breakdown. To some of them, a distinctly premodern form of theology must be reasserted in order to preserve the Christian tradition in the bleak aspiritual world of postmodernity. To others, even modern theology retains too many foundations, implicit or otherwise, and a truly postmodern theology can only be forged with the new tools that the post-Nietzscheans have provided for us. Modern theology, in other words, can be seen as a necessary course correction in the intellectual journey of the Christian tradition, or as a disastrous capitulation to the essentially secularizing tendencies of Enlightenment and post-Enlightenment thought, or, perhaps, as merely the hors d'oeuvre at the banquet of postmodernity, following which the deaths of the biblical God and the god of the philosophers will be served up.

The camp of the radical postmodern theologians is the one with the fewest tents. It is not difficult to see why this would be so. Traditional understandings of God, and even less traditional formulations of God as "ground of being" or "lure of history," are rightly perceived by both post-structuralists and deconstructionists to be foundational principles of the world which, for them, must be supplanted. So, like Nietzsche before them, they understand "God" as the supreme organizing fiction of the Western world and, rejecting that world, they no longer need the fiction.

Actually, what is most surprising is that there are any theologians at all to be found in the camp of the radical postmoderns. As a matter of fact, the very notion of the "death of God" need not lead to a postmodern outlook at all: it could very well portend the intensely subjective self-concern of classical atheism, itself a quintessentially modern phenomenon. What seems to carry certain theological work[2] beyond this point and into genuine postmodernity is what I can only call a nihilistic mysticism. For such thinkers, the removal or "death" of God can lead to the release of a fuller and deeper sense of the religious. Thomas Altizer will dwell upon the connections and even identity between crucifixion and resurrection, or genesis and apocalypse in the light of something like Friedrich Nietzsche's idea of eternal recurrence.[3] Mark C. Taylor, as befits his close affinity to the work of Jacques Derrida, is far more consciously combative not only of traditional notions of religion, but also of the modern picture in which "the creator God dies and is resurrected in the creative subject."[4] The truly postmodern thinker like Taylor must assert that the "death of God," the supreme author, if it leads only to the creative subject, continues to exclude the encounter with difference and otherness. But the brilliant and incantatory word-spinning that follows casts a spell which continues the illusion of religiosity, if not piety.

At the other end of the spectrum of postmodern theologians, we find those who are frankly alarmed by postmodern culture, but whose tendency is to blame modernity's destruction of a prior harmony for the weakness that postmodernity exploits. These are not fundamentalist thinkers. They are, rather, theologians who are frequently fully conversant with the products of both modern and postmodern thought, secular and religious, consciously "writing against," to use Harold Bloom's phrase, the influence of at least some of their intellectual ancestors. Here we need to locate two somewhat different schools of thought, the influential "postliberal theology" of Hans Frei, George Lindbeck, and other representatives of the so-called Yale school, and the "countermodern" theology of the Anglican theologian, John Milbank. While the former group is perhaps less nostalgic than the latter individual, at least over the demise of Christendom, they each in their different ways are convinced that "secular" thought adulterates the gospel. They also believe that the fullness of the gospel demands either something like a premodern understanding of the integrity of the Christian community (in Milbank's case) or the recognition (in the case of the postliberals) that Christianity meets no other group, religious or secular, on equal terms in open dialogue.

Between the radicals and the nostalgics, as usual, we find the pragmatic theologians. These, aware of the negative consequences of an uncritical adoption of the Enlightenment spirit, are also understandably wary of incorporating the death of God too literally into their religious vision. They are soft-core postmoderns. They are comfortable with postmodern themes like the privileging of nature over history, the marginalization of "linear" teleology, and the end of all but metaphorical notions of immortality. But most (James Gustafson is an exception here) would draw the line at eliminating all notions of divine agency, and would want to preserve some sense of "God" as not simply identical with the universe or nature, while not outside it. While they accept the biblical, Lutheran, and perhaps even Hegelian tropes of the "death of God," the Nietzschean remains indigestible, and the Derridean may not even pass their lips. Their engagement with postmodern thought is genuine, which renders their faith more fragile than that of the nostalgics. Their preservation of hope in the postmodern world is a counterfactual commitment to transcendence; thus they are more vulnerable even than the radicals, who have put their trust in the play of the text.

Three sets of theological questions will be examined in the following pages, in each of which the dialogue between some or all of the above thinkers reveals a particular challenge for the postmodern Christian. In the first place, the traditional theological category of the "doctrine of God" undergoes the most serious scrutiny in postmodernity, precisely because of the implications of modernity's struggle with subjectivity. To the premodern or nostalgic postmodernist, the question of subjectivity is unproblematic. God's aseity makes God subject. To the late modernist, a revisionist approach to Kantian transcendental subjectivity, made necessary by the recognition of a thoroughgoing historicity to all categories of thought, leads to considerable theological creativity. Intersubjectivity and communication models of trinitarian thought vie for attention with questions about the nature of Christ's selfhood and depth-psychological assessments of the being of God. Subjectivity is both a stimulation to creativity and an agonizing theological problem. Finally, for the radical postmoderns, the dissolution of the self is the fuse that ignites the explosion of all traditional theological categories. If "I" am not "I" but Michel Foucault's triply doubled self, then what are the implications for the God in whose image I am supposed to have been fashioned?

A second theme worthy of examination is the question of the role of the Christian community in a pluralistic society that accepts some form of moral relativism as a matter of course. This raises again the question of truth, now in a postmodern context. In a world that is merely ethically pluralistic, religious perspectives can compete or collaborate with other religious views or nonreligious views, attempting to persuade the dialogue partner of the value of their particular ethical outlook. This challenge is one familiar in the modern world as a whole and in the United States in particular. But when ethics is undermined by aesthetics or irony, when the very notion of authority is removed from ethical discussion, when truth itself becomes a problematic category, dialogue may seem to become impossible. While we could attempt to address this question by examining the notions of morality proper to different schools of thought, a better and more concrete way is to look at the faithful sociality characteristic of groups that reflect one or other understanding of the postmodern outlined above. In the way in which each group as a religious group engages the secular world we may find a clue to its practical contribution to the development of a postmodern religious ethic.

In the third place, contemporary Christian thought must confront its own version of the problem of otherness. Admittedly this issue could be raised on a number of levels. Racism and sexism are far from unknown in the Christian tradition, and overcoming them is certainly a form of the problem of otherness. It is not, however, a form different in any real way from the way it challenges culture as a whole. For that reason, I suggest approaching the question of otherness by attending to Christology. Confronting the other as other, as we saw at some length in chapter 1, is precluded if we possess a commitment, explicit or implicit, to some master narrative. None is more powerful, nor longer-lived, than the Christian narrative of salvation history, in which the God-man Jesus Christ plays the supreme role of redeemer. How, then, we may ask, do postmodern theologies, respecting the otherness of the other, finesse the question of Christology without abandoning the central significance of Jesus Christ for their religious self-understanding?

The theological dialogue with postmodernity is in some respects more radical than its philosophical counterpart. This is true first in the rather commonplace sense that, religion being what it is, there is more at stake in any significant challenge to it. Religion has always been thought to be about "eternal" truth, and there is something destabilizing for religion in postmodernity's preference for ways of seeing over truth. But if religious thought can get beyond the tradition-bound preference for notions of absolute, unchanging truth, the challenge unfolds even more dramatically. Placed in question are bedrock assumptions about the relationship of God, the world, and the human beings within it. Above all, religion must face the question, What happens to the religious worldview when the human subject is decentered? When anthropomorphic language about God is rejected, when anthropocentric assumptions about God's agency and the teleology of history are put aside, when traditional understandings of immortality, grace, and salvation are queried, religion can perhaps be forgiven for alarm, though not for following the example of the ostrich.

By way of illustration of the degree to which theology must change, let me offer a few reflections on the religious response to postmodern science, building on the brief note at the end of chapter 1. From a religious point of view, postmodern science offers a few clear guidelines for what directions theological inquiry may take. For example, our knowledge of the physical universe has now made it incontrovertible that the human species is interconnected with and indeed dependent upon all other life-forms, and even the inorganic world. In all but the most trivial senses, we are one with our universe. As a consequence, anthropocentric views of reality are no longer theologically justifiable, and while theocentric views may continue to be acceptable, they may not be envisaged in anthropomorphic fashion. Theologies of redemption that see them as a reality offered only to the human race, and not something integral to the entire universe, including whatever other "alien" life-forms there may be out there, are inadequate. Those that focus on the redemption of the individual are positively harmful. Christologies that imagine Christ as less than cosmic are merely parochial. Theologies of the church that stop at the political, still more so those that remain ecclesiocentric, fail because they cannot conceptualize Christian discipleship as in the service of a sick planet.[5] Eschatologies that imagine that the spiritual can have a reality aside from the material are simply naive.

God: Decentering the Human Person

It is my conviction that if we choose to use the analogy of agency for construing the Deity, it must be developed with great circumspection. Insofar as the analogy leads us to assert that God has intelligence, like but superior to our own, and that God has a will, a capacity to control events comparable to the more radical claims made for human beings, the claims are excessive.

—James Gustafson

In Jeffrey Stout's somewhat unkind remark that Gustafson's God seems, in at least one respect, more like a dog than a human being, there lies some truth. Gustafson illustrates well the quintessential postmodern attitude to "God." Whatever "God" is, it is not to be conceived of in anthropomorphic terminology, or even, more radically, to be spoken of analogically. Nor is it the God of revelation, since "revelation" is simply one time-conditioned, culturally formed expression of belief about what Helmut Peukert calls "the whither of transcendence."[6] In Peukert's hands, God has become a preposition, but that is what happens, and perhaps must happen, when the theologian simultaneously rejects biblical imagery and anthropomorphic language. Gordon Kaufman is similarly evasive, defining God in terms of function. For Kaufman, God is:

> that reality, *whatever it might be*, orientation on which evokes our human moral and creative powers (that is, our distinctively human powers), encouraging their development and enhancement by promising significant human fulfilment (salvation) in the future.[7]

Returning to Gustafson, we reenter the world of prepositions. If God is a whither for Peukert, for Gustafson God is a whence, the whence of "the powers that bear down on us and sustain us," in his much-quoted and sometimes vilified formulation.

The status of "God" in contemporary theological dialogue is a fine test case for religious attitudes to postmodernity. While the word *God* is, as Tillich put it, an empty symbol, the Christian community inherits it with considerable accretions, product of three millennia of faith development and piety. Further, the tradition is not only wholly and perhaps inevitably enmeshed in the anthropomorphic language of the biblical heritage and the analogical language of theological commentary upon it, but also reflects an entirely premodern cosmology and anthropology. While the initial chapter of Genesis has God openly declaring an intention to make human beings in the divine image and likeness, it is quite clear to theists as well as atheists that the obverse is in fact also true. The biblical God is made in the human image. But the human image whose reflection this God is must be recognized beyond dispute as a premodern conception. Consequently, much contemporary religious thought finds intensely problematic a presentation of God in the categories of premodern anthropology, and a view of God's universe that is Ptolemaic at best.

Among postmodern theologians of all types, there are *no* thinkers who would defend the accuracy of anthropomorphic imagery about God. There are, however, significant numbers who want to maintain its continuing usefulness, and even its inevitability. In a similar fashion, most if not all would accept that the biblical picture of the God-human/being-world relationship is both a mythical and a narrative expression of religious truth. But there are wide divergences of opinion over what this implies about the continuing centrality of scripture and the peculiar authority of "revelation."

The debates over "God" within the contemporary theological academy seem to involve at least four distinct standpoints, though all four accept in major part the reality of the postmodern world and the intellectual revolution that has transformed, if not finally ended, the project of modernity. At one end of the spectrum we find those like Mark C. Taylor, Thomas Altizer, Carol Christ, and Sharon Welch who, while continuing to speak for the importance of religion, see no further use for the notion of God. A second group, among whom must be counted James Gustafson, Gordon Kaufman, and Maurice Wiles, are deeply critical of inherited understandings of God, finding them inadequate to belief within the contemporary world, but continue to want to use the word *God* in significantly different ways, and on the whole seem to expect a future for organized Christianity. In a third constellation are such as David Tracy,[8] Sallie McFague,[9] Jürgen Moltmann, and Peter Hodgson,[10] who draw on substantial elements of postmodern culture and thought but remain wedded in important ways to biblical revelation. Finally we find those, like George Lindbeck, the late Hans Frei, Ronald Thiemann, and John Milbank whose "postliberal" or "neo-Augustinian" standpoints incorporate a willingness to utilize postmodern thought in tactical or pragmatic ways, but show considerable resistance to any wholesale or programmatic dialogue with the secular world.

Each of these four groups can be challenged in different ways. The first two groups are the radical postmoderns, the one needing to show what remains religious about their perspective, the other what is left of Christianity. The third group, who have most affinities with the late moderns of chapter 1, need to demonstrate how they have made real advances beyond the deficiencies of modern thought and why they need not adopt the radicalism of a Kaufman or Gustafson. The final group have to defend themselves from the accusations of neoconservatism, fideism, or, in the language of the previous chapter, a postmodernity that is really a nostalgia for a premodern world.

What is at stake in this discussion is the reality of God. At one extreme, of course, not even the most traditional of theologians would attempt today to argue that God is an object in anything like the way that we or the World Trade Center are objects. God does not have objective reality in this sense. Having laid the obvious to rest, however, what remains is complex. What does it mean to say that God is real? At the very least, it has to mean that this nonobjective existence of God is still independent existence, in particular an existence independent of the human need for a God, or even of the human imagination's postulation of a God. While human experience may reveal large sectors of potential tragedy or lack of meaning in individual and social existence, and while the religious imagination may arrive at a notion of God to compensate in some way for the darker side of life, if God is real then God must in the final analysis be perceived as acting in some way in or upon both nature and history.[11] While the particular conception of God that we possess is truly a work of the imagination, as Kaufman insists, God in self cannot be a product of the imagination if theism is to continue to mean something different from atheism. And a God who is simply invoked to make sense of the otherwise senseless is nothing more than a Kantian postulate.

In his work on theocentric ethics, James Gustafson illustrates particularly well both the sensitivity with which the discussion must be conducted and the dilemma of postmodern God-talk, the horns of which are encrusted with the blood of many an unwary theologian. For Gustafson, our religious plight today is that we utilize a Ptolemaic religion within a Copernican universe. Those more attuned to science than Gustafson might prefer to say that we utilize a Newtonian religion within a post-Einstein universe. Scientific knowledge, Gustafson reminds the reader, tells us that the human race is not the purpose of the universe, that the universe itself will exist for a finite time, that life became possible only because of the chance concatenation of multiple circumstances, and so on. But monotheistic religious thought, even at its most sophisticated, continues to operate with a view of God as a moral agent. God is taken not only to act like the human person—at least in terms of moral impulses and virtues—but also to be acting on the universe for the sake of human persons. Theologians, thinks Gustafson, while they are mostly ready to recognize that the anthropomorphic God is just a way of talking, and that anthropocentric religion is problematic, cling to a teleological understanding of divine activity and to theological concepts like "salvation" that simply do not make sense outside of the mythical frame of reference.

Gustafson's proposal to rethink both theology and ethics in a theocentric perspective means in essence that all anthropomorphism must be removed from the theological understanding of God, though of course the symbolic value of certain traditional formulations may persist within "piety." So, whatever is said about God must be at least scientifically plausible, though only through the eyes (or better, perhaps, the heart) of piety will its full significance be appreciated. Just as the findings of science have long precluded belief in a three-tiered universe, so they also do not allow the religious person to find solace in a teleologically ordered universe, or in a God who attends to every hair on the head of each human individual. But in the sunshine of what science does not actually preclude, piety may continue to make hay.

More specifically, Gustafson reworks traditional understandings of God as creator, sustainer, judge, and redeemer. The idea of God as creator becomes "human consent to the powers that have brought life into being,"[12] while sustenance and governance are transmuted into "the perception of an order or ordering process,"[13] though one that can be held by someone (like Gustafson himself) who prefers to be agnostic on the question of teleology. When we arrive at a sense of moral accountability through perceiving the adverse consequences of certain actions and relations, this is what corresponds to the symbol of God as judge. Finally, the presence of the redeemer is sensed in those moments of hope and possibility where human agency "can rectify the effects of fatedness."[14] In sum:

> "God" refers to the power that bears down upon us, sustains us, sets an ordering of relationships, provides conditions of possibilities for human activity and even a sense of direction.[15]

While for more radical postmoderns like Mark C. Taylor the death of God is the liberation of religion, Gustafson is not ready to let go of God. But the God to which he clings, curiously for one who insists on the end of anthropomorphism and anthropocentricity, is one conformed to the patterns of human perceptions. The "power that bears down upon and sustains us" is the object of "piety," understood as "an attitude of reverence, awe and respect."[16] But what isn't clear in Gustafson, and is not going to be clear in one who relativizes the previously privileged source of scripture and the general notion of revelation, is whether the piety is a response to an experience of God, or whether God is invoked in order to satisfy the need for the affectivity of piety to have an object.

Gustafson himself recognizes, in his discussion of God as judge, that the symbol of God is not necessary in order to develop that moral sense that there are adverse consequences to certain courses of action or certain types of relationship. Adding that "explanation is not the point of such religious symbols," he goes on: "Their meaningfulness is within the context of a religiously affective response to events and of a theological construal of them."[17] We could say the same for "human consent to the powers that have brought life into being." Such consent does not require the symbol of God, though the symbol will occur to one whose piety predisposes him or her to this kind of explanation. Unless, of course, the piety is a response, not to the experience of powers, but to the encounter with a God who acts first, who speaks first, who takes the initiative. But *that* kind of God is not available to one, like Gustafson, who denies the notion of divine agency.

Gustafson's form of postmodernism is probably the hardest of all to maintain. To be a Mark Taylor or a Thomas Altizer is relatively straightforward. God is dead, but the religious sense remains. But to be Gustafson, you have to believe that God is very much alive, while accepting no recourse and finding no grounds to say anything about God that one might not also say from an atheistic perspective about one's sense of the power of the universe that keeps us all in being. Confronted with this nature mysticism in Christian dress, one is reminded of that Hegelian phrase from the previous chapter, the "finite mind shouldering an infinite task," and in its bleakness and overwhelming challenge one can begin to see why some of Gustafson's acutest critics have called him Stoic.[18]

Along with the abandonment of an anthropomorphic image of God, Gustafson relativizes human hope and purpose. It is not that they are irrelevant to human history, of course, or even to God, but rather that they may very well not be central to "God's purposes" (a phrase that the deanthropomorphizing Gustafson is still inclined to use). The human task is rather to find our place in the general picture of cosmic harmony and to consent to what we discern of the will of God, "a will larger and more comprehensive than an intention for the salvation and well-being of our species, and certainly of individual members of our species." A theocentric ethics is, then, an ethics in which "we are to conduct life so as to relate to all things in a manner appropriate to their relations to God."[19]

In Gustafson's picture, the decentered human being confronting the deanthropomorphized God is challenged to consent to that which is, as perceived through his or her affective experience. Now this is itself not at all unreligious; quite the contrary. Gustafson is saying that God is ultimate, not human beings, and his prayer must be: "Let God be God." Indeed, it exhibits striking similarities to the message of the biblical book of Job, as God speaks out of the whirlwind, castigating both Job and his friends for their requirement that God fit their human categories, and insisting that God's designs are out of all proportion larger than human minds can comprehend. Job's recognition that he has had too much to say and his conclusion, "I will be quiet," seem to be much the kind of consent that Gustafson advocates. Substitute for the classical picture in which God can be an actor, the contemporary silent God who is discernible only through the processes of nature, and the differences between the two are hard to find.

The problem with Gustafson's "consent" to a God of nature is that while it has some religious parallels, it has equal similarities to distinctly nonreligious thought. Compare this recipe of consent, for example, to Nietzsche's demand on the lips of Zarathustra, "Be faithful to the earth!" found in the opening pages of *Thus Spake Zarathustra*. There isn't all that much difference between Nietzsche's view and that of Gustafson. Both oppose anthropocentrism and the role of traditional religion in maintaining it. Both substitute a stoical view of cosmic harmony and a call for a kind of consent as the way to a self-fulfillment that consists in accepting one's place as an individual and the place of one's species in a much larger picture. While their congruence doesn't go all the way—Nietzsche would presumably reject language about "the power that bears down upon us and sustains us"—their similarity is sufficient that it leaves the question whether Gustafson's search for a theocentric ethic hasn't left him outside theism. Who is right, the theologian who announces that "the chief end of God may not be the salvation of man,"[20] or the poor Polish rabbi in Elie Wiesel's *Night*, who knows and recites the message of Job's God that "man is too small, too humble and inconsiderable to seek to understand the mysterious ways of God," but then rejects just such a God?[21] Nietzsche's atheist doesn't face despair, of course. Despair only confronts the one who tries to believe in a God who doesn't make any difference.

This particular reading of Gustafson focuses the issues very sharply. Isn't it the case that the kind of understanding called for in the postmodern world leaves two and only two clear options? Either one must abandon the God of revelation and find oneself in the postmodern desert, in which case it at least makes sense to be there in good faith, along with Taylor, Altizer, and company. Or one must—while accepting the purely mythical character of the anthropomorphic God—find a way to assert a moral purpose in a God, and even a kind of centrality for the human race in God's "plan," and thus demonstrate a God who is more than nature. And doesn't Gustafson's position leave him somewhere between the two, open to criticism from both sides?

Gordon Kaufman's work, which offers an at least equally sophisticated and rather more moderate version of Gustafson's project, namely, to continue to talk meaningfully of God in today's world, evinces a number of similarities to *Ethics from a Theocentric Perspective*.[22] First, he is equally of the opinion that the idea that God acts *as a person*, exercising something like human agency, is no longer viable. Second, he rejects the dualistic vision of a God who is wholly other, entirely outside the universe. Third, he grants no special status to biblical revelation. It is simply an imaginative construct, a creation of human beings in their attempt to express the meaning of "God" that is in most respects no longer helpful. The two reasons for rejecting an appeal to revelation or to any other authority, says Kaufman, are that "for the Christian symbol-system God alone is the ultimate authority" and, striking a more anthropological and less theological note, that "at any given time it is always an open question whether the conceptions and values and perspectives inherited from the past remain suitable for orienting human existence in the new present."[23]

Despite these substantial similarities, Kaufman's project is both less radical and more subtle than that of Gustafson. Gustafson wants piety alone to sustain an impersonal, almost deistic God who "bears down upon and sustains" the universe, but who pays particular attention to no single part of it, still less to any single individual. Kaufman, in contrast, prefers to use the term *God* only to refer to some aspect or feature of existence whose functions are reasonably similar to those of the creator/lord/father of the tradition, and also continue to be important to human life. He rejects the "piety/intellect" dualism of Gustafson, and argues that the imaginative reconstruction of the "image-concept" of God needed for today's world is essentially the same process as that employed in previous times. "The symbol 'God,'" he says, "has always functioned . . . as the focus for a worldview."[24]

The task of theology according to Kaufman is then to engage in an imaginative exercise to construct an image-concept of God adequate to the complexity of contemporary human experience. In this enterprise, written revelation must be allowed no a priori authority, since it is a record only of a previous imaginative exercise. Moreover, the dualisms of traditional theology must be utterly discarded. There seems, he says, no good reason to postulate the existence of an other world or afterlife, except on the basis of the scriptural texts, whose authority is simply their own assertion of such a belief. While we must be aware of the ways in which mystery surrounds all that we can say about religious realities, we have to restrict ourselves to speaking "only in terms of *this* world."[25] Such restriction on speaking is not secularism, since we know that the world is constantly open to criticism and can always be more. But at the same time we need to avoid the reification of the ideal in some postulated other world.

Kaufman's "image-concept" of God is the product of reflection upon the world as understood through the findings of postmodern science. The heart of Kaufman's proposal and much of his originality lies in determining that human life and nature are created and sustained by the "serendipity" of evolutionary and historical processes.[26] "God," therefore, is the name we assign to these processes. While we recognize the laws of entropy in the universe, these processes always demonstrate a "more," a surplus of meaning in which we can locate the genuinely creative in our world. It is this, we might say, in which we "live and move and have our being." This God is at the same time an ultimate point of reference, so in a sense transcendent, since everything else must be understood in relation to it. But it is neither outside the world, since it is our imaginative construction, nor is it "something 'in' the world or a part of the world."[27] Moreover, as our imaginative construction, we must refuse to reify it, though as transcendent it stands in judgment over particulars in our experience. In the final analysis, it must be flexible and revisable; in this sense, it is "the living God."

Kaufman manages to put more space between his God and the atheist than does Gustafson, but at a price. Kaufman's believer puts faith in the serendipity of nature and history, which is surely more than a true secularism can manage. While this may seem both right and attractive at the level of universal claims about "God," however, in particular contexts it may demand either considerable existential courage or profoundly counterfactual hope. Kaufman couples his belief in the serendipity of the evolutionary-historical process with discernment of certain "directional movements" or trajectories, which taken together result in the human valuation of the development of historicity as "good." While he is careful not to suggest that there is some causative agent impelling the forward and upward march of evolution, both in a natural and a "biocultural" form, Kaufman undoubtedly sees faith in "God" as involving a commitment to the potentialities revealed in the a posteriori discernment of this trajectory. This is, I take it, some kind of theological valuation of the anthropic principle. It is a position relatively easy to hold when life is good and the bills are paid. It is even possible to imagine and to promote a stoical or Taoist perseverance in this truth when the individual comes up against existential crises of one kind or another. But what consolation does such a picture offer to the masses of contemporary humanity, daily facing a struggle for survival, watching helplessly the death of their own children and battered by the implacable and relentless forces of nature *and* history?

The major problem with which Kaufman leaves us is the impersonality of the God discerned in the serendipitous creativity of the universe. In the abstract, of course, this is not a problem, since anyone is entitled to believe in whatever God they find compelling. But in the concrete circumstances of Christian traditions, the abandonment of some kind of at least "quasi personhood" represents a deeply radical divergence from the tradition. Obviously, much in postmodern thought moves the theologian in such a direction. Rightly rejecting anthropomorphism as anything more than a way of speaking, and an outmoded one at that, the theologian obviously finds the attribute of personhood to be a ripe candidate for an early trip to the guillotine. The deconstruction of the text collapses the authority of revelation. The all-powerful God of the tradition is a prime example of the evils of untrammeled subjectivity, obliterating otherness, buttressing all kinds of dualisms and promoting false consciousness. But at the same time, a personal God is an enormous consolation, a source of strength and courage in face of life's vicissitudes, and an affirmation of human dignity.

The ghost of Nietzsche hovers over these tumbrels. Once the head has rolled and the cheering died down, there is a great void to be filled. Nietzsche refuses to fill it, and the most radical of postmodern religious thinkers go along with him, proclaiming the death of God. What remains difficult to discern is to what degree those like Kaufman and Gustafson, for all their unabashedly religious sensibilities, do not in the end fall into this same camp. Both would, I am sure, resist being placed in such company. Both can point to elements in their respective bodies of work—Gustafson to his recourse to "piety," Kaufman to the category of "mystery"—in order to reclaim their places within theology proper. But without the element of the personhood of God, they may rightly be charged with having stepped outside theism. And they may, of course, have rightly stepped outside it. Can you, in the end, have theism without anthropomorphism?

Two postmodern theologians who would certainly claim that Christian theism is possible without anthropomorphizing God are Sallie McFague and Peter Hodgson. Both have great sympathy for the kind of project that Kaufman has undertaken, though both have somewhat different concerns. McFague's central preoccupation in her most recent work is with a theology of nature, while Hodgson has lately been preoccupied with a theology of history. They share with one another and with Kaufman a sensitivity to the interconnectedness of nature and history. But they part company with Kaufman in their common concern for the personhood of God. Here, I believe, we encounter theological analogues to the late modern philosophers of chapter 1, thinkers who are aware of the negative side of modernity, and who have internalized its critique of subjectivity, but who nevertheless remain committed to a postmodern reappropriation of subjectivity. Without subjectivity and personhood, they insist, there is no relationality, no divine agency, and, ultimately, no Christianity.

McFague's resourceful attempt to finesse the problem of a "nonanthropomorphic personhood" in God is achieved by way of arguing that the God–world relationship is best understood as a blend of two distinct models.[28] Thus, combining "the organic (the world as the body of God) and the agential (God as the spirit of the body)"[29] makes for a doctrine of God that does no violence to the perspectives of contemporary science. McFague recognizes that the second "agential" model raises the specter of some personal language, but will not bow entirely to science. In a loose application of the anthropic principle, she argues that if we are truly a part of our world, then we need "personal, organic" models and not merely mechanistic models, in order to feel included. Her suggestion is that "we think of God metaphorically as the spirit that is the breath, the life, of the universe, a universe that comes from God and could be seen as the body of God."[30] Such an image is cosmocentric rather than anthropocentric, focusing on "the wonderful life that has emerged from evolutionary history, rather than on the divine ordering of the process."[31]

Hodgson comes to similar conclusions from a more explicitly Hegelian and less single-mindedly ecological perspective.[32] Hodgson asserts that while God is not "a" person, God is "*the* person, person-*hood*, since the power that God has absolutely is the constitutive power of personhood." So, God "is not a finite subject, but infinite subjectivity—which is really intersubjectivity, a communicative interplay of subjects."[33] The justification of this claim is worked out in a depiction of the Trinity as "a triadic, social holism" in which God, world, and Spirit are the "I, You, We" of the Trinity, and "'Spirit' is the most adequate name for the truly infinite and whole God."[34]

Both Hodgson and McFague represent the God–world relationship in panentheistic terms. In the postmodern perspective, this is entirely understandable, even unavoidable if a simple dismissal of the God-concept is eschewed. On the one hand, the conception of the divine existing somehow in a realm of reality totally distinct from that of the universe is precluded, because of the philosophical and scientific problems that such a dualistic vision creates. On the other hand, a simple identification of God with nature renders God impersonal, removes all meaning from any talk of divine agency, and replaces the choice of belief/unbelief with that of optimist/pessimist. Are the facts "friendly," or not? In Hegelian terminology, the choice between a "bad" because it is incomplete, infinite, and the night "in which all cows are black" (Hegel's contemptuous dismissal of Friedrich Schelling's pantheism) is—to abandon Hegel's words—to be between the devil and the deep blue sea. Hodgson and McFague, and even Gustafson and Kaufman, take up the challenge. Those who come closer to meeting it (in my estimation that means Hodgson and McFague) forge theologies in which priority goes to the Spirit, both human and divine. Spirit-theologies allow for the incorporation of the world into God, and the continuing presence of God in the world. But the problems such a view leaves with us are also substantial. A God who is somehow completed in and through nature is one whose sovereignty is compromised, while the role of Christ as the redeemer is definitely marginalized.

Christian Dwelling in a Decentered World

Today it is not nearly enough to be a saint, but we must have the saintliness demanded by the present moment, a new saintliness, itself also without precedent.

—Simone Weil

In a world in which the master narrative of salvation history is more or less taken for granted, the importance and the role of the Christian community is secure. Whether in the more sacramental understanding of the church stressed in Catholic traditions, or the more evangelical vision of the Reformed churches, the faith community is in possession of a truth to which others do not have the same access. At its best, this sign of God's favor is an election to service and responsibility; at its worst, it is a justification for triumphalism or self-righteousness. In either case, the Christian community considers itself possessed of a wisdom that others do not have, and which it is charged to represent in, or represent to, the world as a whole.

Postmodernity challenges almost every element of this picture of the role of the faith community. In the first place, "master narratives" exclude the other, imposing a context-dependent interpretation of reality and, in the case of a religious vision, vesting it with a revealed certitude that can only intensify its oppressive elements. Second, while postmodern individuals may have their own ethical absolutes, if they have not succumbed entirely to the aesthetic substitution, typically they do not recognize the notion of an external moral authority. As a matter of fact, this is increasingly true even for many Christians, who select "cafeteria-style" from among the moral and doctrinal teachings of their tradition those elements that they find valuable, rejecting those they do not. Third, there is a crisis of confidence among many Christians themselves about the appropriateness of presenting their religious or ethical vision as universally relevant in an intensely pluralistic world. Fourth, for many postmodern individuals, non-Christian and Christian alike, Christian moral authority has for too long championed destructive and oppressive versions of reality. Its dualism has long precluded a healthy understanding of the human person and a proper concern for temporal rather than extratemporal reality. Its anthropocentrism has blinded it to the essential interconnectedness of living and nonliving elements of reality. Its deep roots in European culture and the white races, buttressed by a particular "manifest destiny" reading of God's charge to Adam and Eve in Genesis, have meant that its vision of history is one-sided and oppressive. For all these reasons and more, the moral authority of the Christian community in the postmodern world is limited among Christians and almost nonexistent outside them.

Christian responses to the crisis precipitated by the culture, science, and philosophy of postmodernity are quite varied. One obvious path is that of the simple reassertion of traditional beliefs and values. "Family values" rhetoric as employed by conservative American Christians is nothing more nor less than the attempt to shore up a way of life against the corrosive effects of postmodern culture by retiring into an untenable defense of what are often impeccable moral values. The same might well be said for much of the moral teaching of the Vatican, and certainly for the arguments expressed in John Paul II's major encyclical letter on moral authority, *Veritatis splendor*. Both fundamentalisms, biblical and ecclesial alike, fly in the face of postmodernity by asserting an external authority (scripture, church) as witness to the absolute value of particular moral attitudes.

Christian traditions that eschew the fundamentalist option may well want to engage the postmodern world, but for the reasons mentioned earlier any posture of dialogue with that world would have to involve the abandonment of many cherished assumptions of traditional Christianity. Those groups that may have succeeded, at least in part, seem to have done so through the adoption of models of "faithful sociality" that are more recognizably postmodern. Among these would have to be counted the various forms of liberation ecclesiality associable with the base Christian communities of liberation theology itself, and analogous developments within feminist, womanist, and *mujerista* movements, some African American and African theologies, gay and lesbian liberation communities, and so on. We also need to consider here those forms of faithful sociality implied by a postliberal theological vision, or by the countermodern ecclesiology of John Milbank, though the absence of specific communities to which we can point suggests a need for some kind of thought-experiment, extrapolating from the theology to the implicit ecclesiology.

In the remainder of this section of the chapter I propose to examine the forms of "faithful sociality" that follow from the liberation, postliberal, and countermodern positions. I shall try to determine the particular ways in which they might interact with postmodernity, and the implications that each might have for the notion of a postmodern Christian living. In this investigation I want to reintroduce the notion of decentering that we have already encountered so frequently. The Christian church is decentered in the postmodern world, and human beings have been decentered from cosmic history both by the implications of much postmodern science and philosophy and by the work of contemporary Christian theologians. To be Christians in a postmodern world, then, is to be decentered as Christians, as human beings, and in a lesser way and for many of us, as white, or male, or otherwise privileged.

The Christian churches are now decentered in almost every society, though the variety of forms this shift of social position takes is considerable. In some contexts, Christian communities exist with more or less total freedom within largely secular societies (Sweden, England, Germany). In others, they retain considerable status at least culturally, while having lost most if not all of their erstwhile power and influence (Italy, Spain, Ireland, and many Latin American societies). In some places they are still severely restricted (China, Vietnam, Albania, North Korea, Cuba). Ironically, the churches probably occupy the strongest position in the United States, the first nation in the world to pronounce the doctrine of separation of church and state. But even here their grasp upon the collective imagination is waning.

Liberation Movements

An ecclesiality of decentered indwelling marks the self-perception of the base Christian community movement, both in its origins and greatest flowering in certain Latin American societies, and in other grassroots church movements that have grown up in its shadow. Among these one would principally have to include the various forms in which feminist Christians have come to gather together, whether under the "Womenchurch" designation or in some less formal way. To them should be added organizations of gay and lesbian Christians, particularly from the Roman Catholic tradition in this case, where the condemnations of officialdom have only exacerbated their social isolation. And to these, perhaps, we might add numbers of disaffected liberal Christians, though their connection to the perspectives of liberation theology is far more tenuous.

The ecclesiality of liberation theology is distinguished by several factors.[35] First, the communities are composed of those who are marginalized in some significant way, either because of their poverty, gender, sexual orientation, race, age, or a combination of two or more of these classifications. Second, they have relatively well focused group profiles. They are communities that know why they exist, and that express this purpose as a blend of spirituality and social praxis. Third, they de-emphasize hierarchies. Fourth, their theological reflection is context-specific, inductive rather than deductive. Fifth, they tend to oppose dualisms, whether that of nature and supernature, nature and history, salvation and liberation, the Jesus of history and the Christ of faith, the knowledgeable and the ignorant, or the church and the world. Sixth, they have as many, if not more, contacts with non-Christian groups sharing their particular stigma and the social agenda that follows, as they do with mainstream churches and churchpeople. Finally, increasingly and most importantly, they sense the value of cross-fertilization between the different groups that share this liberation family resemblance. Thus, the movement is toward an interactive network of grassroots communities, each constituted with its particular identity and marked by its context and history, yet each willing and able to collaborate with similar groups precisely because they share the same vision of the future.

Perhaps we might call the social vision and eschatology of the liberation communities the "new" society, in the same sense that we have come to talk of the "new" history. Just as macro-level history revealed very little about the lives of ordinary people, and also fell into the fallacy that world-historical individuals and large-scale institutions make history, so there has been a tendency to identify and understand society through some collective ethos of normalcy or decency that existed nowhere but in the minds of the abstractors. Reification of particular understandings of human nature, male and female, and so on, buttressed the typically deductive approach that has held sway in the ethics of Christian institutions, ignoring both the variety of human experiences and the complexity of the individual human life. A similar privileging of already privileged interpretations of Christian symbols has simply tended to ignore the wisdom enshrined in popular religion and the genuine theological insights of the untrained.[36]

The utopian hope of liberation communities is in consequence expressed much more in terms of a new earth than a new heaven. When the traditional biblical values of the kingdom of God are viewed through the lens of liberation analysis, they become a recipe for the healing of a society that makes it harder and harder to be human. The systems-imperatives of modern society tend toward the eradication of difference, and the structures of resistance to the systemic are not well developed in "advanced" industrial societies. Certainly the mainstream churches seem largely unable, or perhaps unwilling, to voice effective protest, tainted as they often are by that kind of compromise with civil institutions and everyday moral values that Dorothee Soelle so aptly dubbed "necrophilia."

Though it is not often noticed, liberation theology and its sister movements incorporate a critique of modernity. The challenge to the church is expressed against the totalizing instincts of traditional theology and the theologico-cultural hegemony of white/patriarchal/ Roman/Eurocentric ecclesiality. The challenge to the secular world is aimed at a whole panoply of factors—geopolitics, free market economics, Eurocentrism, scientism, technologism, and economism—which together represent the metanarrative of the West. Both, religious and secular, reflect the dark side of modernity's triumph in the West. The alternative vision that liberation theology proposes is centrifugal, grass-roots-oriented, community-based, nonhierarchical, intersubjective, devolutionary, in a phrase, "small-scale."

While liberation thought reflects the small-scale, devolutionary, and intersubjective emphases of postmodern social thought, it also has the potential to extend its critique of modernity to challenge the darker side of postmodernity itself. As we noted in chapter 1, Habermas and others have argued that postmodern culture is a product of neoconservativism, which rejects modernity's celebration of autonomy and its championing of human and civil rights. Preferring a vapid amorality, it promotes materialism, consumerism, and social and political indifference, often dressed up with the rhetoric of "traditional values." Radical religious thought sees at least some truth in the Habermasian version of postmodernity, and maintains a commitment to the articulation of meaning and value that, while it is voiced in postmodern communities and alliances, leaves it with at least one toe, if not a whole foot, well within the sea of Enlightenment values.[37]

The faithful sociality of liberation-style communities is then one which both mirrors the best of postmodernity while challenging the worst. The modern moment within the postmodern is what enables it to be critical and indeed prophetic in the face of the excesses of postmodernity, an exercise of that creative out-of-tuneness with the times that Johann Baptist Metz has called "productive noncontemporaneity." But the postmodern moment, in its turn, facilitates a self-criticism about the tradition's inheritance from the past. The churches must proclaim the gospel *anew*, but it is the *gospel* that they must proclaim anew.

The term "faithful sociality" which I have coined to summarize the ecclesial way of being of Christian communities is intended to highlight the two dimensions of this life. "Sociality" stresses the inevitably social and political presence of the members to one another and within the larger society. But the qualifier "faithful" reminds us that spirituality is as important as political praxis. In recent years, Latin American theology of liberation has stressed spirituality much more than in its earlier days, though as long ago as the immensely important meeting of the Latin American Bishops' Conference in Medellín, Colombia, in 1968 both bishops and theologians were pointing out that without *metanoia* a successful revolution against an unjust regime would lead only to the replacement of one tyranny by another. But perhaps the theology of the African American churches is the best example of an essentially liberationist perspective that has always maintained the priority of spirituality. Only such a stress on the importance of interior dispositions could have kept hope alive through centuries in which meaningful social and political resistance were simply inconceivable.

Postliberalism

Both postliberal Christianity and the countermodern "Christendom" of John Milbank's conservative Anglicanism are more difficult to isolate for examination because neither has inspired distinct alternative Christian communities. Much the opposite is the case; ecclesial and cultural malaise has fueled both theologies. Postliberal thought articulates in academic form mainstream Protestantism's revulsion at the milk-and-water Christianity of its liberal counterparts and attempts to alert the churches to the dangers inherent in mediation and accommodationism. John Milbank's proposals radicalize the postliberals' perspective, eschewing like them any mediating attempt, but going way beyond them to propose a neo-Augustinian model of Christian community as the authentic solution to the problems of the world. Both views deserve to be discussed here, since they exhibit many of the characteristics of postmodernity: a critique of modernity, a strong emphasis on Christian community, and an unwillingness to go in search of the lowest common ethical denominator in the name of dialogue and collaboration either with the secular world or with other religious groups, understood as "ways of seeing what is" (Milbank's phrase). If we leave aside hard-core biblical and ecclesial fundamentalisms, since they are of their nature inimical to intellectual challenge, postliberalism and countermodernism seem to represent the only serious alternatives to a liberation-style ecclesial model.

The *locus classicus* for postliberal theology is George Lindbeck's *The Nature of Doctrine*.[38] While you will look in vain in that slim but influential work for any extended account of Christian community or discipleship, it is possible to construct a view of the role of the church in the world with the assistance of some of Lindbeck's other writings.[39] Indeed, as we shall see, postliberal ecclesiality seems particularly well adapted to the postmodern world.

The fundamental motivation for postliberal theology is to stem and reverse the tide of theological liberalism. In the postliberal view, the strength of the Christian church, and in the end its continued viability, rests upon its maintenance of a clear sense of its own identity. But liberalism, that child of Enlightenment and the fuel that powers modernity, undermines the particularity of Christianity. Typical of liberal (Lindbeck's phrase is "experiential-expressive") religious thought is its inclination to identify religion with feeling. Thus, for the liberals, Christianity is a particular historically and culturally conditioned mode of representation of truth that is the common possession and/or pursuit of all sincere searchers after wisdom. Hence, liberal theology typically employs philosophical, psychological, or social-scientific interpretive models to "mediate" between the Christian message and the wider world. Such a "foundational" approach to Christianity empties out the specificity of the tradition and substitutes a vapid lowest common denominator. In the end, all religions become forms of enjoining the golden rule. In a slightly different formulation of the liberal problem, Stanley Hauerwas argues that liberalism is "particularly pernicious" precisely because "it prevents us from understanding how deeply we are captured by its account of existence." And primary in that account is the conviction that "society can be organized without any narrative that is commonly held to be true."[40]

Lindbeck's "cultural-linguistic" model of religion presents religions as self-enclosed language games in which doctrines operate as grammatical rules. They are, in other words, not transferable to other languages. As a consequence, the members of the particular faith community must understand the world in their own language. Indeed, the limits of what they can think are set by the limits of what they can say. It is in this context that we must understand the much-discussed slogan of postliberal theology, "It is the text . . . which absorbs the world, rather than the world the text."[41] While this can seem to have an imperialistic ring to it, the intention seems only to be to stress that nothing can be understood outside the language we are able to use.

The "text" to which Lindbeck refers is not solely understood as a language, but at least equally as a narrative. The fundamental interpretive schema through which Christians understand the world, of which the language (grammar, vocabulary, and so on) is a reflection, is derived

from the scriptural account of Christian self-identity. Thus, the specificity of the Christian story is the matrix by means of which Christians
interpret and judge the world. While great and constant efforts must be
made to ensure that the Christian story is apprehended in terms appropriate to the times in which the community lives (this is no ahistorical
fundamentalism), the narrative cannot be negotiated away in the service of dialogue or some higher truth, and it cannot be equiparated to
something else, since the only way to do so would be to allow some
other language interpretive priority over the scriptural narrative itself.

Lindbeck's *The Nature of Doctrine* is primarily an account of postliberal theology. It is a polemical, trenchant piece, brushing aside both
"propositionalist" and "experiential-expressive" approaches as equally
unfaithful to the specificity of the Christian narrative. It has generated
wide debate, spawned a number of interesting offspring, and been the
occasion of frankly visceral reactions, incurring charges of ghettoizing
the church and of an ecclesial model reflective more of insecurity and
fear of the modern world than of a bold proclamation of scriptural values. While these criticisms may be wrong, or at least overstated, they
may also be a result of some lack of clarity in Lindbeck's presentation.
For example, David Kelsey's predominantly sympathetic assessment recognizes a problem with the "master metaphors" of culture, language,
and grammar. They may suggest, says Kelsey, that "church life and discourse [are] *in principle* disengaged from, and logically incapable of
engaging in, the public realm." So, the objection that Lindbeck's view is
inescapably sectarian, while inaccurate, may be "rooted in an intuition
about the inapplicability of the metaphor."[42] It also seems to be an over-
simplification and perhaps in some cases a real injustice to accuse experiential-expressive theologians of, however unwittingly, *reducing* the
specificity of the Christian narrative to something else.

If Lindbeck's views of theology leave some questions, as an account
of ecclesial practice his vision of a cultural-linguistic model of the
Christian church has much to recommend it. It seems, in particular, to
be well suited to the devolutionary character of the postmodern world.
When a higher, unitary metaphysical framework is abandoned, and
when the power of the transcendental subject has become the focus of
intense suspicion, fragmentation can only result. When no one notion
of truth or of ethical authority is universally maintained, when con-

text, rhetoric, and cultural conditioning have come to hold sway, narrativity may not be a bad bolt-hole.

Commentators have occasionally noted that there is no identifiable postliberal church, but insofar as this observation is true, it may be a strength, not a weakness. The cultural-linguistic model does not describe any particular Christian denomination, though it can perhaps be said that it cannot coexist with certain perceptions of Christianity—fundamentalism, scriptural or ecclesial, and any profession of Christianity of a pronouncedly pluralistically liberal cast. But it is available to and may be perceived in the perceptions and practices of individuals and of church communities, wherever they rest their self-identity upon the narrative of scripture.

The nearest thing in current Christianity to a postliberal practice is to be found, in fact, in the faithful sociality of churches inspired by the theology and ecclesiology of liberation. This may be accounted a surprising judgment, in view of postliberalism's frequent disparagement of liberation theology. Thus Lindbeck, in calling for a return to "Israel's story" on the part of Christians and regretting that "there are as yet few signs that this is happening," singles out liberation theology for criticism. On the political left, he says,

> liberationists selectively appropriate episodes from Israel's history, especially the exodus, but use these as legitimating precedents for their own campaigns, not as shapers of a comprehensive community of sinners and saints, oppressors and oppressed, tyrants and liberators.[43]

Were such a judgment of liberationists true, the criticism would be fair. In fact, it is a caricature that is both unjust and, more importantly, counterproductive, since it actually prevents postliberal theology from recognizing the existence in liberation theology in practice of a cultural-linguistic model at work.

While we have already said a substantial amount above about liberation theology and ecclesiology, we need here to recognize those elements in it which substantiate the claim that it represents a form of postliberal ecclesiality. In the first place, the ecclesial practice of churches motivated by liberation theology, for example, is rooted in the scriptural reflection of the local believing community, as it attempts to see the practical implications for the life of the oppressed in God's word of liberation, extended to all but in a special, "preferential," way to the poor. Second, while it consciously utilizes social-scientific method and even Marxist analysis, it professedly does not make these foundational to theology, but employs them in an ad hoc, descriptive manner. Third, it self-consciously employs a narrative of the Christian community that stresses its continuity with Israel, in particular with the notion of the *anawim* and with the prophetic tradition, and in the ecclesiality of the base Christian community it looks back to forms of Christian practice distinctive of the early church. Fourth, if we wish for evidence that theology is subordinated to the narrative and to the practice of the community, we need look no further than Gustavo Gutiérrez's often-quoted statement, "theology comes after." It is the "second act" of religious reflection.

Countermodernity

John Milbank's "countermodernity" is more extreme. To borrow from the language of Raimon Panikkar,[44] if liberation theology is an expression of Christianness, and postliberal theology of Christianity, then Milbank's manifesto is a shameless reassertion of the premodern superiority of Christendom. The countermodern ecclesiology was sprung upon the theological world quite dramatically with the publication of his *Theology and Social Theory*[45] in 1990, in which he straddles the issues and debates of postmodernity in a highly idiosyncratic reading of Western civilization. Filled with a distinctly unmodern confidence in his religious tradition, Milbank takes on everyone, from those like Hugo Grotius and Thomas Hobbes, whom he believes carved out the independence of the secular by misconceiving the character of the religious, to the founders of sociology, to G. W. F. Hegel and Karl Marx, and to the idea of salvation at work in liberation and political theologies. Having disposed of the moderns, he turns to the postmoderns, both the hard core of Nietzsche and those under his influence (Gilles Deleuze, Martin Heidegger) as well as those who reacted against him—among them, Jacques Derrida, Jean-François Lyotard, and Michel Foucault. He next deals much more gently with what he calls "benign" postmodernism, particularly the work of Alasdair MacIntyre, Donald Davidson, and Richard Rorty, coming finally to his constructive proposal in dialogue with Augustine and Dionysius.

Milbank's thesis is quite simple. The "nonfoundational metanarrative" of Christianity incorporates a social theory that is entirely adequate to, even vitally important to, our postmodern age, and that is distinctly superior to those secular social theories with which Christianity is thought by so many to need to engage in dialogue. Thus, the work's subtitle, *Beyond Secular Reason*. What so many believe to be the appropriate stance of Christianity in today's world is one of openness toward secular disciplines, particularly those of the social sciences. It is through engagement with the discoveries of secular social science, think many, that Christianity can bring its message into our modern, pluralistic, public arena. This, says Milbank, is quite wrongheaded. While Christianity can utilize the insights of social science, it accommodates itself to the paradigms of secular science at its peril. Christianity does not have to conform itself to the assumptions of the world: rather, the world has to conform to the vision of the Christian tradition. In this analysis, Milbank is obviously not far from Lindbeck and the postliberals.

In the final chapter of his book Milbank considers the construction of a Christian social theory as the explication of the actual practice of the church. Indeed, all theology, says Milbank, must be rethought as the "renarration of practice." To the dialectical history of secular and sacred Milbank opposes an Augustinian reading of the church as the City of God, a realm of ontological peace. In the Christian metanarrative of the genesis of the church, moreover, he sees a renarration of "real" history that incorporates a reading of all history within it. In other words, the Christian metanarrative claims to be an interpretation of universal history. It rejects, he says, the Jewish claim to explain the mysteries of human community and salvation, and he *seems* to say that it must conclude that all non-Christians, "however virtuous-seeming, [are] finally on the path to damnation."[46] He argues that Christianity exhibits "the exemplary form of human community," and thus that it cannot admit that the social sciences might carry out a more fundamental investigation in this matter without abandoning its claim to truth. Christianity, he concludes, makes "a gigantic claim to be able to read, criticize, say what is going on in other human societies," and this "is absolutely integral to the Christian church."[47]

For Augustine, says Milbank, the political community is based on the necessary coercion that must exist in any society in which there is

residual sin, and so it cannot be a realm of justice, whose basis is chari-
ty. Thus the political is imperfectly social, whereas true society, in the
alarming words of Milbank,

> implies absolute consensus, agreement in desire, and entire harmony
> amongst its members, and this is exactly (as Augustine reiterates again
> and again) what the Church provides, and that in which salvation, the
> restoration of being, consists.[48]

Aquinas is consequently faulted for recognizing social and economic
life as natural, as part of a separate political sphere, which can only
lead to thinking of the church in a privatized and narrowly "spiritual"
way. Better to preserve a somewhat fuzzy separation of church and
state, to preclude either "a sovereign state or a hierarchical church."
Then the church as the realm of ontological peace can challenge the
necessity of violence, which is only credible if the social world is natural and separate. The church promotes the "ontological priority of
non-violence, and this way is called 'forgiveness of sins.'"[49] The harmonious consensus that will result "is . . . something like 'the peaceful
transmission of difference,'" discerned not in philosophical reasoning
but as "a claim of faith and experience that that is how this particular
tradition works."[50] Through this praxis the sphere of *dominium*, of the
secular exercise of sheer power, can perhaps be made to recede. The
church will emerge as an asylum from punishment, a "space of just
exchange," and a "sphere of socially aesthetic harmony" in face of the
tragic necessity of *dominium*.

Milbank's vision of the church, if I understand him correctly, identifies it as the one institution and the one tradition in the world and in
the space of human history that can legitimately claim to be a community of peace, the home of Being that includes and celebrates otherness.
His attack on modernism is in the name not of a postmodern "play" or
eclecticism, but rather of a kind of premodern metanarrative of Christian identity that yet shares postmodernism's refusal to disprove the
other through capitulation to some totalizing critical matrix or principle of universal rationality. Thus he can and does assert the superiority
of the Christian community, without ever having to defend his position. He wants to be at once distinctly premodern in his adoption of a

metanarrative, and characteristically postmodern in not needing to defend or prove its virtues over against other options. There are, as he says elsewhere, "infinitely many possible versions of truth," but it is "not quite" the case that "Christianity is just on a level with other . . . discourses." It is special in that it can become "internally postmodern" through its suspicion of fixed essences, and through its pursuit of "a universalism which tried to subsume rather than merely abolish difference." All postmodern discourses are equally postmodern, one might say, but one is more postmodern than the others.

There are undoubtedly some valuable insights within *Theology and Social Theory*, above all perhaps the insistence on Christian theology as the narrative of Christian praxis, though at times the language of description seems to become as dizzyingly speculative as the worst kind of metaphysics. Perhaps this is the "strange kind of return" of a premodern metaphysics that Milbank predicts, one which in the postmodern context is "a necessary 'fiction' concerning the unseen relation of time to eternity, not a record of observation of this relationship."[52] In any case, this attention to practice makes it possible for Milbank to mount a serious attack on the intellectual affinities of liberation theology while singling out the base Christian community as one of the best examples of his vision of the church. There is a problem here, undoubtedly. One would expect Milbank to be in agreement with the Vatican's consistent critique of the "people's church" for substituting conflict for reconciliation. Yet the very base communities he speaks of with approval are primary examples of ecclesial structures which argue that premature recourse to the language of reconciliation hides both the impact of the ecclesial abuse of power and the limited though healthy place of conflict in the gospel.

In the final analysis I have to say that Milbank's vision of the church makes me uneasy. Much of my unease derives from the shaky marriage between the premodern and postmodern. The premodern Christian vision was open to the apologetic dimension, and was able through its espousal of a metaphysic to engage, at least in principle, in dialogue with unbelievers. In this it differed little from modern Christian theologies. But the postmodern perspective has abandoned the premodern and modern, and is content with the play and the trace of the deconstructionist, the genealogies of the poststructuralist, or the neopragmatist's irony. Milbank wants it both ways: namely, to assert the superiority of the Christian metanarrative, and not to have to justify its claims in the open court of reason. While he argues—to some extent rightly—that his position need only be defended, in postmodern fashion, by the explication of Christian practice, the church that he in fact describes, or would describe if his explication went deeper into detail than it does, is a distinctly premodern community.

Hidden away within all Milbank's erudition there is, it seems to me, a kind of ecclesial absolutism, which is where he certainly parts company with the postliberals. While no details are furnished about worship, sacramental life, or even polity, the hints that the author provides suggest a highly structured and settled ecclesial order. He claims that this will be a hierarchy of values rather than of persons, but immediately adds that it will involve the subordination of individuality and collectivity to "a substantive organization of roles, purposes and values."[53] This certainly seems to me to suggest the settled social order in which everyone knows his or her place, and one in which a peace that embraces and perhaps even asphyxiates difference is preferred to the freedom that presumably would lead to honest disagreement and dissent. Moreover, while the idea of a community founded upon forgiveness and eschewing violence is a glorious vision, what Milbank takes to be the practical implications of this should give pause for thought. Thus, he quotes favorably Augustine's doctrine that

> Nothing that properly is, by nature, resists other natures, and therefore one must pass beyond suppression of passion towards the rectification of desire, and a peaceful order that is a pure consensus.[54]

Milbank's attempt to distance himself from Hegel notwithstanding, it seems to me that his social vision of the church is not that far from the Hegelian state which is, in Hegel's words, "the way of God in the world." Hegel's state, which is the embodied ethical idea, is just such a community in which true freedom is the perfect consonance of the individual ethical will with that of the whole. Commentators have often suggested that some at least of the intellectual origins of the fascist state are to be found in Hegel's conception, and while the dialectical vision of history and the stress on individual freedom seem to me to save Hegel from this judgment, I am not sure the same can be said for a scholar who privileges peace over what can sometimes be cleansing conflict. It is not easy to see a place for honest dissent in Milbank's ecclesiology, for all his talk about difference, still less for how someone might honorably walk away from the church. In the religious as in the political landscape of postmodernity, one obvious response to a sense of impending chaos is a turn to totalitarianism, however benign.

Milbank's description of theology as the "renarration of practice" also raises some questions. Clearly his objective here is to overcome the speculative and deductive theologies of premodernity and modernity, and their dependence on philosophical criteria not themselves derived from an examination of Christian practice. I have a lot of sympathy for this position. But by what stretch of whose imagination could a renarration of Christian practice arrive at the conclusion that Christianity is "differences in a continuous harmony"? A renarration that is truer to actual history, I would suggest, both of the relations of Christians with one another and of the contact between Christianity and the non-Christian world would be "savage disagreements, constantly at one another's throats, with the spilling of a great deal of blood." Now of course Milbank does not believe that the Christian community has always lived up to its high ideals, and he even suggests that this "continuous harmony" exists only "in aspiration and faintly traceable actuality."[55] But if that is the case, I am not sure how one can derive this "peaceful transmission of difference" from a renarration of practice. It sounds just a little too much like the idealist's ploy of juxtaposing the "in-itself" to what "it" has in fact usually turned out to be. This way, the "faintly traceable actuality" is classified as the real because it in fact instantiates the idea of Christian harmony. But no genuine renarration *of practice* licenses a claim to Christianity's evident superiority and hermeneutic privilege over universal history.

Privileging Christianity raises yet another question. While I think Milbank may well be on to something in his belief that "secular reason" was a product of nominalist theology (a point also made by Louis Dupré in the book referred to in the previous chapter), and that Western social science is as dogmatic (theological) as theology itself, so that I have some sympathy with his discussion of the relation between the Christian tradition and the Western drift to nihilism, I find his silence on other religious traditions disturbing. When Milbank asserts that the Christian church "claims to exhibit the exemplary form of human community" he does so over against the counterclaims of social science, sometimes admitted by Christians, to "carry out yet more fundamental readings" of history. His argument for his position is cogent and important. But what of all the religious traditions of the world that are quite unaffected by the secular reason of Western culture, that have their own metanarrative and which—as I have suggested above—could make at least as good a case from their renarration of practice for embodying a harmonious community? Milbank's postmodern gambit secures him from the need to engage in an apologetic or polemic in the face of these other options, but—and this he does not seem to see—it also makes the claim to superiority one that he cannot justify. Some difference cannot be included within the Christian harmony, but to our author everything outside the church is error. While his argument may carry some weight in relation to Western society and even other Western religions, it says nothing about non-Western ways. It seems to me that the author owes us the recognition that there are some limits to his ambitions in *Theology and Social Theory.*

Returning finally to the Western world within which Milbank's argument seems inevitably to be imprisoned, his book leaves a lot of questions unanswered. *Which* church is the "peaceable kingdom"? How is an individual excluded or included? What must someone do to be included? Is a secular pacifist outside the church while a violence-prone "Christian" is in? Or is the name of "anonymous Christian" to be bestowed on all those outside the fold who yet eschew violence and thirst for the transcendent? Where is the hunger for peace and justice and—the postmodern God forbid—truth? Isn't there in the end something odd about preferring the peaceful postmodern community focused around a fiction to a thoroughly modern church on pilgrimage, struggling to know the truth, open to the diversity of other peoples and other traditions and what they can offer to the search, yearning for the reign of God? What is catholic, exactly, about Milbank's church?

It is, in the end, quite preposterous to expect the reader to accept the argument that everything outside the church is the realm of power, of sheer *dominium.* Of course, a lot of it is, especially of our everyday public and political life. But then a lot of what is inside the church is an exercise in sheer power too. Milbank expects us to accept that wherever power is found *in* the church it is to be regretted but does not efface the vision of the church as a community of peace. On the other hand, wherever harmony and justice seek to prosper outside the church, for all the good intentions it is inevitably to be accounted in error. There are, however, significant figures who flit briefly across the pages of this book, greater attention to whom might lead to a modification of the absurd excesses of the argument. Richard Rorty's more recent work[56] adopts the perspective of liberal irony, calling for a piecemeal involvement in discourse in the search for contingent responses to discrete situations that demand justice: fiction, in other words, without the metanarrative. In principle, it would seem to me, the absence of metanarrative is likely to reduce the temptation to the exercise of power rather than increase it. Metanarrative itself is a kind of power play. In a different vein, Jürgen Habermas[57] envisages a community constantly engaged in discourse that seeks consensus on the norms for emancipatory action. His communication community accepts the rule that all validity claims must be tested by appeal to evidence, and that every member of the community must be accorded equal access to the discourse. Under these conditions, intercommunication is itself emancipatory, excluding the exercise of power. Both Rorty and Habermas are securely ensconced in the *saeculum*, but all the words in *Theology and Social Theory* are not going to convince me that their work stands at odds with the harmonious reconciliation of differences.

The liberation, postliberal, and countermodern ecclesial visions all have a place here, since all address, implicitly or explicitly, the problem of postmodern fragmentation. Each presents a model for dealing with the decentering of the Christian community in the postmodern age. Moreover, all facing in their different ways the experience of marginality, they make a virtue of necessity. The social marginalization of traditional liberationist communities is understood to give them hermeneutical privilege in interpreting the world, and indeed to make them especially favored by the God who takes sides with the marginalized. The construal of theology as grammar licenses the inward-looking mien of postliberal ecclesiality. Finally, Milbank's countermodern Christendom accepts the isolation of incommensurability and makes it the justification for a nondialogical assertion of superiority, like a little boy under pressure, blindly declaring, "my peaceable kingdom is bigger than your peaceable kingdom!"

The Theology of Religions: Decentering Christ?

Jesus lives in the depths of non-duality—that is, where God, the other and ourselves form only one reality. This is my body, this is my blood.

—Jean Sulivan

The "theology of religions" is a curious term, being used in contemporary theology to refer to religious reflection upon the relationships between Christianity and other religions. We find it, for example, in the title of a 1987 collection of essays edited by Leonard Swidler, *Toward a Universal Theology of Religion*.[58] In the "Proem" to that book, Swidler explains that the theology of religions must include all religions and ideologies, not just Christianity, or just theism, or just religions, and that its intended audience must also be all religious and ideological communities. He implies—correctly, it seems to me—that the possibility of such a theology rests upon a rejection of the total incommensurability of religions and ideologies. A pluralism that can recognize the possibility of a universal perspective must be one that posits some points of contact. But he also raises the perhaps more important question of whether a universal viewpoint can be found from which to do a theology of religions. And this must cause the further question, not addressed here by Swidler, of what it might mean to do a "universal" theology of religions from the perspective of one religion or another. Would not a Christian and a Theravada Buddhist "theology of religions," assuming that the Buddhists were willing to play, be two very different products? And could we imagine a multiplicity of universal theologies of religion, each eschewing the imperialist or exclusivist option, and yet each looking different from the others because of the point of origin? It sounds like a strange project, but one less fraught with difficulties than the impossibility of doing a universal theology from a neutral position. The "universal" perspective is, of course, no perspective at all.

The language of the discussion of other religions focuses around the terms "exclusivist," "inclusivist," and "pluralist." The usual use of these terms is relatively obvious. So, an exclusivist position privileges one's own religious tradition and consigns all others to the flames, sometimes literally. The occasional battle cry of both Catholic and Protestant traditions, "outside the church there is no salvation," is a reflection of exclusivism. The inclusivist option recognizes the values to be found in other religions than one's own, but sees these as inchoate, partial graspings after the truth of one's own religion, or a "preparation for the gospel" (Vatican II's phrase), or evidence of the work of the Spirit (of God) throughout the world. Thus, from a Christian perspective, all other people of goodwill become some kind of "anonymous Christians," in Karl Rahner's characterization. The pluralist view is still more liberal, essentially arguing for the relativization of all religious traditions, including one's own. Each is a culturally and historically bound search for the meaning of life, an expression of the way things are.

The basic uses of these three labels are open to immediate criticism. The exclusivist approach finds itself in the untenable position of arguing that the evident goodness and wisdom of other religious traditions is a chimera, and that countless millions of people who lived exemplary lives have no share in the salvation offered by God. The inclusivist line of thought avoids such crudity but falls prey to the vice of disrespect for the integrity of the other. To tell religious people that we respect their traditions only insofar as they represent an approximation to our own is at best politically incorrect, at worst downright insulting. Moreover, when we start to explain what it might mean to claim Gandhi or the Buddha or Mohammed for the ranks of anonymous Christians, it rapidly becomes apparent that we have to water down the specificity of Christianity in order to accommodate them. The inclusivist school of thought must thus move toward a lowest common denominator of the Christian genius. If anyone who does good and avoids evil is an anonymous Christian, then Christianity is fundamentally about doing good and avoiding evil. The pluralist approach to other religions is able to maintain the otherness of other traditions and the specificity of one's own, but at the price of abandoning any a priori claim to the superiority of one's own religion. Superiority can be established only on historical grounds, and, as John Hick has shown with devastating accuracy, on historical grounds Christianity does not distinguish itself.[59]

In actual fact, the theology of religions debate does become a little more nuanced than the simple ranging against one another of the exclusivist, inclusivist, and pluralist options. In their most elementary forms, all three suffer from serious problems, but hybrids of two of the three produce much hardier strains. Two hybrids are discernible in the postmodern debate. The first is a blending of the exclusivist and pluralist positions, producing a theology that stresses respecting the incommensurability of other traditions while it licenses a concentration upon one's own as if we still lived within the world of Christian hegemony. This view is implied in postliberalism and expressly stated in John Milbank's countermodern strand of postmodern theology.[60] The second is a marriage of the inclusivist and pluralist options, emphasizing the value and richness of the pluralist abundance of ways of wisdom while insisting on the hermeneutical necessity of maintaining a specific, particular, context- and history-bound way into the diversity of religions. Thus, while I do not privilege Christianity in any absolute sense, I encounter other traditions through the lens of my own. I can, of course, change traditions, but I cannot be neutral.

The problem of "other religions" raises in a clear way in theology the concerns over otherness and difference that we encountered at the end of chapter 1. As we saw there, any metanarrative, even one that recognizes the existence of difference, in essence eradicates that difference for the possessor of the metanarrative by including the difference within the metanarrative. The only way to encounter the different as different is through the abandonment of the metanarrative. Thus, for example, feminist thought has been intensely critical of the metanarrative of universal reason, and has argued instead for a model of storytelling in which each distinct entity, community, or individual is given space and respect to tell its story without critical submission to some hegemonic canon of rationality.

The theological variant of this problem of metanarrative and otherness is that apparently the only way to escape hegemony is through the embracing of radical pluralism. But radical pluralism also relativizes one's own story, and it is extremely difficult to reconcile the traditional claims for the person and work of Christ with a vision in which Christianity is just one way among others that human communities have sought to come to terms with what is. All theology is reduced to rhetoric, Christ to a prophet, God to a name for ultimate reality. The church is just a human community, salvation is "reality-centeredness"

(John Hick's phrase), and the sacraments are therapy. But how can Christianity escape such reduction and still allow the other to be other?

Two volumes in the Orbis Press "Faith Meets Faith" series exhibit many struggles with this dilemma. In 1987, John Hick and Paul Knitter edited a collection entitled *The Myth of Christian Uniqueness: Toward a Pluralistic Theology of Religions*, in which they gathered essays that showed "a move away from insistence on the superiority or finality of Christ and Christianity toward a recognition of the independent validity of other ways."[61] Three years later this was countered by *Christian Uniqueness Reconsidered: The Myth of a Pluralistic Theology of Religions*, edited by Gavin D'Costa. This second volume rejects the notion of a pluralistic theology and explores whether "Christian claims concerning uniqueness [are] coherent and sustainable and even illuminating in making sense of religious plurality."[62] Taken together, these volumes testify to the complexity of the issues.

First, it must be said that both groups of participants in the debate accept the fact of Christian uniqueness and the fact of religious pluralism. No one wishes to deny that Christianity, like any other religious tradition, possesses an irreducible particularity, and I would venture to add that the particularity is most securely located in the Christian narrative, not in creeds or lists of doctrines.[63] Where disagreements occur is on the question of the normative character of the narrative, and the narrative's undoubted commitment to the uniquely redemptive status of Jesus Christ. Second, it would be foolish to argue that there is not, as a matter of fact, a plurality of religious traditions and therefore that pluralism is an inescapable characteristic of the religious world. What is in dispute is not the fact of religious pluralism in this weak sense, but the degree to which a stronger claim is being made, namely, that Christianity is to be given no hermeneutical privilege or normative status within this plurality.

The more sophisticated proponents of pluralism do not attempt to deny that Christians will and should continue to view the world through the lens of their particular tradition. Pluralism is not, therefore, necessarily a radical relativism. In Panikkar's words, "pluralism is not the eschatological expectation that in the end all shall be one."[64] So, Langdon Gilkey constructs a careful argument for a "relative absoluteness" in his essay "Plurality and Its Theological Implications."[65] "Ours," he says, "is only one way, and yet we remain there."[66] He argues that to accept the particularity of our starting point is inevitable, since "no universal standpoint, cultural or religious, is available to us." However, the Christian symbols represent "a relative manifestation of absolute meaning":

> Just as any vision of plurality is itself qualified by the affirmation of a *relative* center, so each apprehension of infinite meaning is qualified by and expressed through particular symbols.[67]

Using Christology as an example, Gilkey claims that Christ is the revelation of the infinite as "absolute love, as *agape*," but this does not mean that other symbols from other traditions might not reveal the infinite differently, or even as the same agape.

Raimon Panikkar's lengthy discussion in "The Jordan, The Tiber and the Ganges" is unusual for a pluralistic approach in recognizing the "possible incommensurability of ultimate worldviews."[68] Incommensurability is usually the preserve of exclusivists (Milbank, for example). The river imagery is used in two ways. In one, it is intended to convey three dimensions of the Christian tradition. The Jordan represents the exclusivity of Christianity, the irreducible particularity of its origins. The Tiber is the moment of institution, of mission, and hence of an at-times imperialistic inclusivity. And the Ganges evokes pluralism, outwardness, and the acceptance of the fact of irreducibility and the possibility of incommensurability among the world religions.

But in a second (actually earlier) use of the river imagery, rivers represent religious traditions. Rivers, says Panikkar, are life-giving, but they do not meet, nor need to meet. They only meet, in a sense, in the sky, and the vapor of the Spirit is "poured down in innumerable tongues":

> The true reservoir of religions lies not only in the doctrinal waters of theology; it lies also in the transcendental vapor (revelation) of the divine clouds, and in the immanent ice and snow (inspiration) from the glaciers and snow-laden mountains of the saints.[69]

In a move similar to that of Gilkey, Panikkar finds "the christic principle" to be "neither a particular event nor a universal religion" but "the center of reality as seen by the Christian tradition.[70] It is a universal vision, but not "an absolutely universal one." Perhaps we should say, it is a vision of the universal, but not a universal vision. Were he to argue the opposite, our pluralist would metamorphize into an inclusivist. And this is where the incommensurability argument is important: It renders impossible any collapse into Christian imperialism, and it removes the possibility of any evidence that would license sheer relativism.

If this invocation of incommensurability is important to the pluralist position, then it becomes necessary to ask just how different in the end is a nonrelativistic pluralism from the supposedly opposing position represented by the essays included in the Gavin D'Costa volume. With the possible exception of John Milbank's contribution, this book contains no representative of exclusivism, and the Hick and Knitter text is similarly bereft of relativists. We come therefore to a question of nuances. On the one hand there are those who would argue that utilizing the Christian tradition as the lens through which I interpret the world and encounter other religions is an inevitable hermeneutical circumscription, the "scandal of particularity" revisited, as it were. On the other we find those who, while accepting this inevitability, would like also to talk in terms of the normativity of Christianity, while recognizing that the incommensurability of other traditions prevents any easy descent into inclusivism. They are, in a typically postmodern move, content to live with the ambiguity.

A few examples from the D'Costa volume will illustrate the complexity of the antipluralist position. D'Costa himself makes a case for the normativity of a "trinitarian Christology," but argues that it protects against exclusivism and pluralism, enabling both a pneumatologically driven attention to "the universal activity of God in the history of humankind," revealing love of neighbor (including those of other religions) as "an imperative for all Christians," and licensing praxis and dialogue.[71] John Cobb strongly affirms Christian uniqueness, but also the uniqueness of other religious traditions, and finds one norm that transcends this radical plurality of unique religions, namely, "the ability of a tradition in faithfulness to its past to be enriched and transformed in its interaction with other traditions."[72] And J. A. DiNoia argues that the Hick and Knitter volume is actually unfaithful to the pluralistic project, effectively imposing a "soteriocentrism" on the debate. Thus, he goes on, a truer respect for pluralism would preserve the particularistic claims to universality of Christianity and other religions:

Rather than suggesting major alterations in the world's religious landscape, such proposals would attend to its specific features and strive to
account for them in all their intractable diversity.[73]

Much of the confusion and apparent conflict between representatives of these two positions can be dispelled if we pay attention to
remarks made by DiNoia in the D'Costa volume and by Gordon
Kaufman in the Hick and Knitter collection. DiNoia, generally
thought of as a moderately conservative Catholic theologian, is careful in his call for a true pluralism to point out that he speaks as a
philosopher of religion. In other words, in the essay in question he
has deliberately adopted a standpoint outside his own confessional
perspective. Seated there, his remarks are unassailable. Of course
many religious traditions, including Christianity, make claims to universality. Of course a truly pluralistic overview will respect the particularity of each set of claims. And of course it is an unwise step to
introduce an umbrella term (Mystery or Reality), derived from none
of the traditions in question, in order to assert that all the traditions
are indeed talking about this more fundamental concept. But DiNoia
would be led to different conclusions, I would venture, if he were
attempting a theology of religions *done from the perspective of the
Christian tradition.*

Kaufman's essay, "Religious Diversity, Historical Consciousness and
Christian Theology,"[74] contains implicitly what is essentially the same
distinction to be found in DiNoia's proposal, and one that few in this
debate have recognized. There is a difference between what is demanded of fundamental or philosophical theology on the one hand, and systematic theology on the other. Kaufman rightly sees that most Christian believers and theologians understood the theological task to be "one
of interpreting and passing on [the] truths and values of the tradition,"
and not of "fundamentally questioning, criticizing, or reconstructing
them."[75] Yet, of course, while systematic theology is rightly taken up
with issues of the clarity and consistency of the tradition's expression of
its convictions, fundamental theology has other priorities. It must
attempt to explicate the plausibility and intellectual respectability of its
worldview in categories which, while compatible with revelation, are
not drawn from it.

Interestingly enough, a liberal Protestant like Kaufman and a Catholic like DiNoia would both be comfortable with the notion of differing tasks for fundamental/philosophical theology on the one hand and systematic theology on the other, though they both might have problems with the way in which I have just formulated the distinction. But while the former might need to be reminded that the task of fundamental theology is not quite that of philosophy of religion, since it is inescapably tied to the particularity of a Christian hermeneutic, the latter must be led away from an apologetic or even polemical version of the foundational project. In other words, while systematic theology necessarily proceeds on the assumptions of universality, it need never thematize these assumptions. But foundational theology, which is in the business of thematizing, cannot proceed on the unthematized assumptions of universality that are proper only to the in-house activity of the systematician.

And so we come finally to confront the question of the role of otherness and difference in the Christian perspective, of which the other religions debate is but an illustration. As we have suggested several times, adherence to any metanarrative leads to the eradication of the otherness of the other. But as the debate we have just glanced at has indicated, the adoption of a pluralist position can itself be an unwitting but no less real commitment to a metanarrative, whether it draws on the Western metanarrative of liberalism or it substitutes a Western notion of Mystery or Reality for the particular ultimates of various religious traditions. Are we then forced to the conclusion that the sheer relativism of absolute incommensurability is the only way to preserve difference? And if so, is the price of this not the abandonment of all judgment, the end to true dialogue, and—as Langdon Gilkey so forcefully argued—opening the door to "forms of the religious that are intolerable, and intolerable because they are demonic"?[76]

The way forward may well be through the development of some notions of modified or relative difference, and will certainly involve rejection of absolute otherness. That which is absolutely other is simply and wholly inaccessible to that from which it is distinct. Thus, absolute incommensurability becomes total incomprehensibility. The turn to panentheism, or indeed the trinitarian form of the Christian God, is itself a recognition that the "wholly Other" God of philosophical speculation makes revelation impossible and salvation unlikely. But in the case of the more elusive notion of relative difference, what must be avoided is any sense that differences are relative in relation to some norm, whether Christian or supra-Christian (Reality, Mystery). So perhaps a term like "differences in similarity" or dialectic of difference and similarity might be more useful.

In the end, the best approach might be a blend of the radical feminist rejection of a notion of universal reason, the weak foundationalism of a Habermas, and the Gadamerian concept of "fusion of horizons." So, the feminist contribution would stress that religions, worldviews, and points of view exist in a kind of marketplace of ideas, where the differences and specificity of particular voices must be attended to without any attempt to place them under the judgment of a particular historically conditioned (and perhaps gendered) notion of rationality. The Habermasian would add that as a matter of fact, just such undominative discourse can only occur because of a common commitment to certain formal canons of rationality—truth, truthfulness, sincerity, and so on. And the Gadamerian must insist in turn on a substantive component to the possibility of emancipated dialogue, in the necessary exercise of a fusion of horizons between the world as apprehended by the speaker, and the world as apprehended by the listener.

This formal procedure suggests a way of dealing with the otherness of other religions, provided that we bear in mind that the mode of encounter with them is through fundamental, not systematic, theology. Given the rejection of absolute otherness as implying total incomprehensibility, in the first moment we must encounter the other in all its irreducible difference, yet we can only encounter it at all because its account of experience chimes in to some degree with our own. In a second moment, only formally separate, the possibility of comprehension without incorporation is given in the linguisticality of the communication. Third, and only third, we relate this communication of the other to our own symbolic universe and account of reality, and perhaps thematize those points of connection or convergence that made the initial encounter with the other something different from total incomprehension.

An Agenda for a Postmodern Theology

*I do not feel the peace I once did. Not with God, or the earth, or any-
one on it.*

—André Dubus

The intention of this chapter has been to lay out some of the seemingly intractable problems created for contemporary theology by the intellectual and cultural conditions of postmodernity. In none of the three
debates into which we have entered have we been able to do much
more than uncover the main lines of argument and the logic of different theological standpoints. The doctrine of God, the nature of the
church, and the particularity of salvation in Christ, of course, have
been contentious issues for as long as there has been a Christian community, and the postmodern religious landscape is not different,
because these continue to be matters of dispute, though the way in
which they continue may be and probably is quite idiosyncratic.

Three major theological issues are addressed and left unresolved in
the above discussion. First, how if at all is God to be considered personal any longer, if the anthropomorphic and the anthropocentric are
to be eschewed? Second, what are the tasks of Christian community in
an age marked by pluralism and suspicious of metanarrative? Finally,
can the christocentricity of Christian theology be retained only at the
price of a psychological reduction of salvation, if the church is not simply to revert to cult status? Putting it even more briefly and bluntly, is
there a place any longer in postmodern Christianity for God, Christ,
and the church? And if not, is there really a place for Christianity?

If I am right that these are the issues for Christianity today, then it
must mean that the postmodern theological agenda is apologetic in its
true purpose if not always in conscious intent. This theological work will
be found somewhere between philosophy of religion and fundamental
or philosophical theology, not principally in the domain of systematic
theology. I am content that for *systematic* theology the text will continue
to absorb the world, and the systematic theologian will begin with the
plain sense of the narrative, ending there again in a second naïveté after
the hard work of unpacking the excess of theological symbols has been
attempted. It also seems clear to me that the path of all Christians needs
to be essentially the same one, if they are not in the end to allow the

specificity of their own religious narrative to evaporate. But the encounter with the world that does not accept the privileged status of the Christian narrative is also a profoundly important moment in theology. Here is where apologetical theology is at work, representing Christian understandings of reality as cogent if not necessarily compelling, that is, as not inherently irrational or offensive to basic human sensibilities. But to do its work adequately, apologetical theology must embrace— sometimes critically and sometimes appreciatively—the spirit of the age and the sometimes unthematized convictions that ground it. An agenda for a postmodern apologetics, then, will seek ways of representing God, church, and Christ in categories that are amenable to the age without being unfaithful to the cherished religious vision of Christianity. A sketch of some ways to approach this will be the objective in the third and final chapter of this book. But before we turn to try to meet such a challenge, we ought to remind ourselves that a *postmodern* theology will at least to a degree reflect the open-ended, pluralistic, pragmatic, and tentative nature of the postmodern world. A couple of pages back I described the problems we are about to address again as "seemingly intractable." It is not the project of what follows to solve them, but per- haps to learn, utilizing Frank Kermode's instructions on reading a classic text, the art of "responding creatively to indeterminacies of meaning inherent in the text and possibly enlarged by the action of time."[77]

3

A Postmodern Apologetics

Apologetical Theology: The Moment of Mediation

If there are always in Christianity latent virtualities which each age discovers in proportion to its needs, one may hope that from the great movement of thought in our time there will emerge, little by little, the philosophical form which is in keeping with its religious requirements.
—Maurice Blondel

Foundational (or fundamental), systematic, and practical (or pastoral) forms of theology are equally important moments in the theological enterprise, but they do not all play by quite the same rules, nor use the same languages. What is usually called systematic theology, for example, is a "moment" of theology internal to the faith community, in the sense that it is not directed to others, though it will of course bear traces of the age, share in historical conditioning, and be even consciously formulated with an eye to the world in which it is being fashioned. At the same time, in systematic theology it is within the language derived directly from revelation and the dependent narratives that the meaning of the tradition is explicated for those committed to it. If there is any part of theology in which the postliberal claim that "the text absorbs the world" is true, then it is here. What is often known as foundational or even fundamental theology is quite a different enterprise, however.[1] Here, where the theological traditions of the faith community are expressed in a language that is not derived from the tradition, we encounter a hermeneutical, dialogical moment best understood under Hans-Georg Gadamer's conversational rubric of the "fusion of horizons."

In the fundamental, hermeneutical, apologetical moment in theology, the fusion of horizons occurs within the consciousness of the theologians and religious thinkers. The world questions the text (or narrative), and the text responds, adding its question in turn. This kind of theologian—in whom text and world meet—must speak the language of the tradition and the language of the world in which that tradition is to be represented. Neither language is to be preferred to the other. To lean toward the secular is to engage in reductionism; to favor the sacred is to absorb the world into the text once again. Both extremes misunderstand the enterprise of this kind of theology, which is—to repeat— the representation of the tradition in categories not drawn from within the narrative of the tradition itself. Apologetical theology is the moment of theological outreach to the wider human community, and needs mediation if its message is to be heard. But at the same time it brings secular wisdom to the aid of the faithful community itself (*fides quarens intellectum*). Thus, the theologian taken up with this fundamental moment will be deeply immersed in the cultural and intellectual processes of the age. Cynics might consider this today to be a thankless task, but it is the only way in which mediation can occur. Others, most notably the postliberals, reject such mediating or foundational theology altogether. But it will be the argument of this portion of our text that while there is much wisdom in the call for the faith community itself to attend to the plain sense of the narrative, the call of the church to mission cannot successfully be communicated without a mediating or foundational moment in the theological enterprise.

What "wisdom of the age" is discernible in postmodernity? While there is obviously much debate about this question, our investigations above have resulted in a modest but significant harvest:

1. No standpoint is neutral or above suspicion. All are rhetorical.
2. Metanarrative erases otherness by including the other within "my" metanarrative, thereby removing its otherness.
3. The task of understanding or interpreting society, if attempted at all, must be conducted through piecemeal, tactical, pragmatic, and tentative means. The philosopher must be the *bricoleur*.

4. The task of changing society, if attempted at all, must be conducted through grassroots, localized (though sometimes networked), tactical, pragmatic, and incremental means. The social activist must be committed to dialogue and consensus building.

5. Postmodernity contains within it elements both emancipatory and demonic. No theoretical grid is available that will easily allow the discernment of which elements are which, though the kinds of totalizing impulses that would reject points 1–4 provide important hints.

While it is pointless to make the claim that these five insights represent the whole or even the center of postmodern wisdom, it is not unreasonable to assert that they are at least an important part of what postmodern thought has discerned in its times. If so, then apologetics has a gargantuan task. Traditionally, Christianity has always made a strong claim for the superiority of its account of reality, for its uniquely saving significance, and for the absoluteness, not relativity, of its claims to truth. In the more critical and rational age of modernity, Christianity in both Catholic and Protestant forms evaded the problems raised by its convictions through claiming for itself a realm exempt from science and reason. But postmodernity's critical reappraisal of modernity has destroyed the possibility of such a continuing evasion, paradoxically, by wiping out modernity's claim to scientific accuracy, objective truth, and universal reason, and by reinscribing mystery—and hence religion—within the everyday world.

To make the claims I have made above about the wisdom of postmodernity is itself to stake out a position within postmodernity. This position is not finally compatible with either of the types of wholesale rejection of modernity itself. Both the nostalgic countermodernism that employs some aspects of postmodernity in the search for a renewed premodern security, and the radical postmodern rejection—celebratory or Stoic—of any humanism at all must now be left behind. In the end, the former would relinquish modernity's hard-won freedom of the human person to some larger synthesis, while the latter surrenders the difficult task of justifying social responsibility to a radical individualism assuaged (in some instances) by an irony that can have its source only in guilt or loss of nerve.

If this were a secular work and I were a secular thinker, then the middle-ground, "weak" reading of postmodernity I would espouse might best be seen as an upbeat reading of Jürgen Habermas's position. What Habermas seems to me to have done in his more recent work is to reaffirm once again the Enlightenment view of the human person, but to represent it as a challenge, as a counterfactual philosophy of humanity, as a target at which to aim. The triumph of freedom, autonomy, justice, and so on are victories still to be won, and whether the struggle will be successful or not is an entirely open question. But the process by which human society could assert the priority of the human over the instrumental is in place. Debate, conversation, dialogue, consensus, and so on are all skills that are in principle available. Whether or not they are employed will be a matter of the human will to overcome structural constraints.

At the present time, in Habermas's view, the prospects do not look good. The system has all but triumphed over the more human imperatives of the life-world. The usual interpretation of Habermas's pessimism identifies the culprit as a neoconservative manipulation of the "system" and the consequent preponderance of instrumental over communicative action. But a second and perhaps equally important explanation lies in Habermas's belief that while the countercultural (hence, countersystemic) forces at work within society possess powerful critiques of the system, they mostly fail to articulate a *program* for an alternative society. Now while the first explanation can be seen as a sober assessment of the power of the enemy, the second is not so simply dealt with. What Habermas identifies as a failure of vision may well seem to these grassroots cells of the "postmodernism of resistance" to be a healthy rejection of metanarratives. Moreover, might they not charge Habermas himself with reneging on his commitment to a *discourse* ethics and a communicative praxis?

There seem then to be two impulses at war with one another in Habermas's attitude to postmodernity, and the resolution of the conflict may be instructive in our task of a postmodern apologetics. On the one hand, he proposes a thoroughly tactical, tentative, and pragmatic approach to problem-solving in his theory of communicative action. On the other, he relapses into a thirst for the implementation of grand visions that could not comfortably coexist within an ethics of discourse and consensus. Another kind of grand vision is implicit within his communicative action theory, however, namely, a philosophical anthropology of the human person as oriented toward truth, comprehensibility, sincerity, and ethical behavior, and hence toward the construction of a community that reflects such beings. If Habermas can be seen in this light, then he must be accounted a champion of a "metanarrative of the human person" which leaves open all decisions about the kinds of actions that the community of discourse might determine.

The question for apologetics in face of postmodernity might be posed in the following way: Is it possible to understand the fundamentals of Christian theology as lying *behind* the human person and the community, so to speak, forming the rhetorical background out of which the tradition encounters the world, rather than placed *in front of* the person and community, as a blueprint for history or a program for the reform of the world? If such a self-understanding is acceptable to the Christian tradition, then it removes the dogmatism that precludes any serious engagement with the non-Christian world, religious or secular, as equal partners in dialogue. With such a view, the Christian narrative would make us who we are as we engage in discourse with the multifarious communities and interest groups that make up the postmodern world. But it would not of itself foreclose possibilities about the direction in which consensus might be found, or the shape of a social praxis that might emerge from the discourse.

Within the apologetical moment of theology, on this understanding, theological statements are not claims about the way the world is or should be, but rather about the ways in which we are as individuals and as faithful communities within a wider world of which we are inescapably a part. They articulate the difference that we bring to the encounter with the other, just as inescapably fashioned into who she or he is by the traditions that lie behind her or him, and whom we meet on the level playing field of our common humanity. Thus, with our narrative which is explicitly not a metanarrative *behind us*, we engage with others who arrive similarly equipped. Indeed, the test of willingness to abide by the canons of communicative action is a blend of the degree of freedom we feel from the compulsion to incorporate the other into our narrative, with the level of openness to the otherness of the other to which we can commit. We are very clearly who we are because of the Christian narrative that has shaped us. As adult individuals formed by our traditions, we are precisely free individuals able to enter into an open encounter with the other or a process of dialogue on ends to be achieved, without being constrained to do either through the lens of a metanarrative projected in front of us.

If we are able to countenance such an understanding of the product of fundamental theology, we must be able to show how the fundamentals of the narrative can function so as to clarify our own sense of who and how we are without clouding our relationship to the world which is not us. This, to my mind, is the major task of a postmodern theology, since the postmodern world is inescapably pluralistic, and we are inescapably a minority within it. Moreover, our options for the future seem only to be three. We may embrace the totalizing discourse of the "end of history" proponents, in which case we lock ourselves once again within Western models of progress and the good life. Or we may let our plurality become further fragmentation and even disintegration. Or we may in our pluralistic world join one another in piecemeal collaboration (bricolage) in the name of a somewhat better world. This third and final possibility is not merely the only one that a Habermas could countenance; it is also the sole option for the kind of person and the kind of community shaped by the Christian narrative.

In the remainder of this chapter we need to draw some lines in the theological sand. What kind of God, we must ask, is compatible with the Christian narrative and yet makes us a faithful people able to engage the postmodern world in the way I have outlined above? Second, we need to examine what kind of community we must be to be able to shoulder this task of mission. And third, perhaps most difficult of all, we need to know what understanding of Christ and the universal salvation he brings can shape us and our community for free and open discourse with those to whom Christ is quite irrelevant. As we proceed in this endeavor we shall be seen, I hope, to be achieving some resolution of the debates we have outlined in chapter 2. How can a personal God be maintained in a profoundly nonanthropocentric and nonanthropomorphic fashion? How is *faithful* sociality possible in a non-Christian world? And just how can the Christian tradition adhere to its narrative in a nondominative fashion?

God: The Relief of Anthropocentrism

Suddenly everything went still as though some coded message had made listeners of us all. I heard something moving on the opposite bank. But then I wasn't sure. I held my breath to hear better. Deer? Raccoon? The great horned owl? The creature tongues resumed and I strained harder at the silence behind them. Then I knew I would never know.

—James P. Carse, *Breakfast at the Victory*

In both the "plain sense of the narrative" and the traditional theological approaches of Christianity, God is a problem. Try as we might to demythologize the biblical representations, God is in some sense standing outside the world, yet exercising an influence upon it, indeed, intervening in the world in quite decisive and disruptive ways. Of course, most theologians today do not tie themselves to literal readings of biblical events, but most do not feel free to contradict the overall structural understanding of a God who is wholly other yet in relation to the world. Put as succinctly as the tradition permits, God always was, is, and always will be creator.

In the light of postmodern understandings of the human person, and especially in view of the convictions of postmodern science, the contemporary fundamental theologian can no longer credibly talk about God as God is presented in these texts and traditions. Certain inescapable truths, once unknown but now clearly seen, have changed forever the landscape in which theological work must be done. For one thing, given the knowledge of the size and scope of the universe, and the clear logical and existential possibility that there is life elsewhere in the universe, all Christian cosmologies and their attendant anthropocentrisms are undermined.[2] Second, with the terrifying awareness that human life as a whole is fragile, and that there is a logical and existential possibility that the human race could destroy itself, most probably through nuclear war or environmental collapse, notions of providence must be radically redrawn. Third, the special claims for the Christian narrative of history, juxtaposed no longer to sin and error but now to postmodern difference, seem far less compelling.

There was a time, of course, not long ago, when to raise issues such as these would have invited the immediate and possibly accurate charge of rationalism. It seems entirely probable, however, that where the theologians of modernity were guilty, to a degree, of trying to bring the gospel into line with a world without much mystery at all, the theologians of postmodernity are attending to something very different. The traditional understandings of God do not allow for the degree to which radical, even absolute, mystery is now found *within* the universe. So, at the beginning of the twentieth century, the belief that the mediating theology of Protestant liberalism was guilty of such emptying out of the specificity of Christianity was a principal motivation for the rise of neoorthodoxy. At the close of the century, what postliberal theology—the late century form of neoorthodoxy—has to confront is not the propositional or even experiential-expressive form of thought that it usually challenges, so much as newly emerging postmodern mysticisms that find more than enough mystery within the universe for the religious imagination to grapple with.

Such developments seem to explain the contemporary attention to panentheism and Spirit theologies that we noted in the previous chapter. Both these approaches attend to the presence of God within the world in a far more generous way than traditionally sectarian readings of the Christian God, and in a bold rejection of both "death of God" and "a/theology" motifs. But they also bear witness to the continuing concern of these postmodern believers, which they hold in common with their more traditional brothers and sisters, for a God who is mysterious, who is more than the sum total of what-is, and who is yet in relation to the totality of what-is. Postmodern theologies of this kind are most emphatically not reductionistic. They remain a little too much within traditionally evangelical understandings of the role of religious conviction, however. That is to say, at least as illustrated by the work of representatives like Sallie McFague and Peter Hodgson, the narrative creates a religious landscape within which the individual moves. However generously, the religious position operates *in front of the believer*, as a hermeneutical grid within which everything in reality will find its place.

The postmodern determination to represent God as other yet as interested and involved takes Catholic form in the sacramental phenomenology of Jean-Luc Marion.[3] Marion subjects the entire ontotheological project of modernity to a radical critique. All special metaphysics and ontology, even the subtlety of Martin Heidegger's ontological difference, effectively makes the image of God captive to a particular philosophical conceptuality, thus reducing God to the status of an idol, that is, a product of the human mind whose end result is to create a mirror in which the believer sees self, not God. To this, Marion juxtaposes a phenomenological view in which human listening, or attention, allows for God's self-communication through an icon. The icon (for Christians, of course, this means above all the icon of Christ) is the transparent means by which God communicates with the human being. It is a one-way communication in which God is revealed as gift, or better as "giving," thus without content, and most certainly without the content of being or Being. But while Marion's approach deals an effective blow against the philosophical hubris of modernity, it leaves us with too little God to believe in. Or it would, if Marion did not finally identify his philosophical work as merely the outlining of a possibility, made actual only through revelation. His fundamental theology is only a natural theology, in other words, and he must retire into revelation to fill out and specify the austere phenomenological concept of contentless giving.

David Tracy suggests a more liberal Catholic approach to the relationship of otherness and agency in his notion of the "mystical-prophetic" trajectory. Tracy introduces this idea into his discussion of George Lindbeck and Hans Frei, arguing that "the dialectic of prophetic and mystical readings" of the tradition provides for organizing the multifarious possible readings of the "plain sense" advocated by the postliberals.[4] The attention to mysticism justifies the orthodoxy of mystical—even apophatic—approaches to God, while the stress on the prophetic keeps alive for Tracy the importance of human agency. Thus, mysticism is not necessarily quietism and the prophetic is not mere activism. If Tracy is substantially correct here, then the God who lies behind the Christian encountering the world is one who is mysterious, largely unknown, and yet also familiar and even intimate, while at the same time enabler of and cheerleader for human agency. The many ways of reading "the plain sense" thus become ways of talking about these two more fundamental categories through which the Christian and the Christian community are to be defined. But none of this involves invoking a God who does more than offer communication at the deepest levels or support the free agential activity of human beings.

Approving of Tracy's position as I do, it becomes important to indicate the differences between what he has to say and where I shall shortly end up. Tracy is characteristically generous in his inclusivity. While concerned to identify his own position, and that which he values most, as a correlational one, he is also at pains to find room for many others, including the cultural-linguistic model of postliberal thought. So the mystical-prophetic dialectic becomes an overall rubric for many theologies, some of which might not altogether be comfortable with the bedfellows Tracy has assigned to them. For my part, the God who is met mystically and the God who inspires free human agency is also a critical construct that presses certain conceptualizations of God or human activity further back into the myth, and excludes them from the moment of apologetical theology in which the conceptual content of Christian tradition is opened to non-Christian and nonreligious symbolic universes.

In seeking a postmodern God-concept along the lines I have indicated, I find myself drawn to the Hebrew Bible, and specifically to the book of Job. There are three "Gods" in Job. There is first the petty tyrant of the legend, who all but destroys Job in order to prove to the avenging angel that Job's love for God is disinterested. The second God is present in the consciousness of Job's friends and Job himself, though in the mind of the author, this God is absent from reality. This second God is the God of the theology of retribution, the awesome judge who stands ever-watchful and who daily blesses the good with material rewards and inflicts horrid ills upon the sinful. The third God, the God of the whirlwind who speaks to Job is—at least for the author, and eventually for Job—the real God, a figure infinitely more terrifying and believable than either of the other two.[5]

The God of the whirlwind is anxious to correct human misunderstandings, and to provide information about the true face of the divine. At one level, God speaks out to challenge assumptions about the accuracy of human images for approaching the reality of God. In a sense, this is God indicating the analogical nature of religious language; God does not conform to the human pattern of a just judge. Hence the friends are wrong to accuse Job of sin because he is apparently being punished, and Job is wrong to demand that God should behave like the just judge God is supposed to be. At a deeper level, this is God denying the reality of the theology of retribution, and hence destroying the traditional connection between virtue and material prosperity, between sin and misfortune.

When the God of the whirlwind breaks the age-old conviction of the relationship between virtue and reward, vice and punishment, this God is also erasing the traditional understanding of providence. In effect, God is denying that God's providential care over creation, whatever it is, implies intrusive and constant attention to the predicament of each individual. Yet the God of the whirlwind by no means denies a relationship to creation; quite the contrary. God is the God of all creation, and is indeed constantly taken up with a providential care of the whole. God has a responsibility for each and every moment and item within creation, from its beginning onwards, but the pattern of this relationship is not adequately captured in any formulation that implies God's caring is apportioned differently between different human individuals, or between the human and nonhuman inhabitants of our world.

If God's care is a care of the whole, indiscriminately and with no favoritism, then from the point of view of any human individual it may seem like no care at all. It is a far cry from God's providence as creating and sustaining the whole, and hence every part of the whole, to God looking out for me, protecting me from my enemies, and so on.[6] But from the point of view of the whole, if the whole were possessed of consciousness, it might seem like the most secure form of care imaginable. Now of course the problem with all this is that the whole precisely does not have consciousness, while human beings do. Thus is theodicy born, as Moche the Beadle in Elie Wiesel's *Night* might say, by asking the wrong questions. "Why me?" assumes a God who makes just the kinds of distinctions in providence that the book of Job rejects.

If God's relationship to the universe is understood on the model of the God of the whirlwind in the book of Job, then the clear consequence is that human agential activity is enormously important. The less God's providential actions are understood as directed toward the fortunes of particular individuals, and more to maintaining the whole in its integrity, the more the fortunes of individuals need to be understood in terms of their own actions, the actions of others upon them, and the unpredictability of circumstance. The old saw, "Pray as if everything depended on God, but act as if everything depended on you," becomes a programmatic utterance. In the religious context of a hope in God's care for the whole, but cognizant—in the classic mystical formulation—that "the only eyes God has are our eyes, the only ears God has are our ears," we step boldly and optimistically into an open future, yet one in which our individual fortunes, and the continued health of the human race, are not guaranteed.

Let us now turn back from the ancient classical profundities of the book of Job, in which a sublime but difficult notion of God's providence is maintained, but in which Job at least has the assurance that he has heard it *from God*, to our own more tentative and insecure age, in which we wish to maintain a similar God-concept in the context of God's silence. Here I think we can proceed in a kind of reversal of Marion's statement about *his* God-concept, that it is suggested by philosophical inquiry but confirmed through revelation. Scripture, it seems, suggests as one model among others the understanding of God I have derived from the book of Job. But postmodernity, seen in the light of Bertolt Brecht's remark about science limiting our error rather than prescribing our knowledge, confirms this particular notion of God as that which is compatible with the Christian life of faith in our times. There is an extremely strong compatibility between Job's God and a notion of God with which a believer can engage the contemporary world. There is no need to maintain an intrusive understanding of God, arranging the personal destinies of individuals on a daily basis, no need to suggest that the Christian is located any differently from the non-Christian, religious or not, in face of the demands of praxis in our world.

We have heard in the book of Job just what it must be like for God to be God. There are those, indeed, who find God to be bullying Job with an account of God's responsibilities. But how can we construct for an age in which God is silent a parallel account of what it must be like for God to be God? All we have said so far has been from our point of view. Even when we have been at pains to stress the nonanthropocentrism of the divine, it is we who have been saying it. When we have puzzled over what it must mean for God to be in any sense personal, it is from *our* understanding of person that we have started and, too often, to our understanding that we have returned. We would certainly be ill-advised to try to put ourselves inside the mind of God, since, as the God of Job might say to us, the only result of that would be to put God within our own minds and reduplicate the errors of anthropocentrism.

We might start along the perilous path of looking at things from God's point of view by enunciating the rather unpromising truism that if God is God, then God is the God of this universe, not of some other. God's care for this universe will then, if God is God, take the form of responding to the particular characteristics of the universe that actually exists. Vis-à-vis human beings, this seems to me to have two important consequences. First, as we have noted several times before, human beings have neither reason nor right to claim to be the meaning of the universe. And second, which we have not previously enunciated, human beings seem by nature to organize their entire environments around themselves.

It may be that for this God we are imagining, human beings are an ornament of particular beauty in the universe, though if this is so then one might well begin to wonder about the divine taste. But there is absolutely no way in which they can be considered necessary to the universe. At this stage of human evolution the universe as a whole is modified in no appreciable way by the existence of human beings, and the planet on which they live is affected, if at all, only negatively. Human beings are then just a part, and a small part at that, of the whole that is the particular object of God's care. Nothing, other than our own hubris and the possession of consciousness, justifies human inclinations to place themselves at the summit of the "divine plan." But hubris is not worth comment on, and the possession of consciousness could only be employed to glorify humanity if there were absolutely conclusive proof that there is no conscious life anywhere else in the universe. Absent that proof, the consciousness argument is itself simply further hubris.

At the same time as we have to argue, however, that God's providence does not single out human beings, since God's care is for the whole universe, we are quite justified in maintaining that from God's point of view, the particular character of the care must be modified to suit the needs of this or that object of care within the whole. From God's point of view, then, the care of human beings will take a form dictated at least in part by their possession of consciousness, insecurity, real but defective rationality, emotional life, and, most importantly, a dynamism toward greater perfection. A rose is a rose is a rose, but a human being can get better or worse. So from God's point of view, what form should providential care take if it is to respect the particular character of this real but totally unnecessary component in created reality?

John Hick's "Irenaean" phrase, "the world is a place of soul-making," nicely captures the quality of postmodern divine providence. It is because human beings possess possibility as a distinctive mark of their species and their species alone, coupled with their equally idiosyncratic faculty of consciousness, that God must be present in the mode of absence. The divine hand must be stayed from interference in the fortunes of individuals, if individuals are to have a chance of becoming more of what their innate potentiality for growth promises. Such a religious judgment coincides exactly, though it does not agree, with the atheistic conviction that religious belief is inherently alienating. Sigmund Freud, Karl Marx, and Friedrich Nietzsche are quite correct, of course, given the God-concept with which they work. But the notion of God enunciated in Job and derived again from the consciousness of the postmodern age escapes the judgment of the masters of suspicion. God is most definitely not an amalgam of human qualities. God is misconceived if imagined as one who would free human beings from the facts of fate and mortality. This God who stands behind the believer and the faithful community impedes in no way the involvement of one or all in the hard work of doing justice and building utopia, and does not have the kind of moral agenda that would license the substitution of an ethic of obedience for truth to self.

If God is present in the mode of absence, however, then this is no mere absence, but an intentional absence. God is present in the intentionality of the decision to be absent. If postmodernity is right to insist on the inescapably rhetorical, context-dependent status of all agents, then the same is going to have to be said of God. If God is God, we might say, then God alone is the possessor of the standpoint of universality. Perhaps we could speak rhetorically of God as the universal standpoint that legitimates the radical relativity of all human standpoints. From that universal standpoint, as we have already noted, God perceives the minor place human beings hold in the universe, alongside their bottomless capacity to interpret it as a very major place, indeed to see themselves as the hermeneutical key to the universe. God's care of this universe, tailored to the needs of each component within it, is truly the meaning of providence. And the particular character of the need that the human component possesses can be named love, as Christians have for so long proclaimed. It is the love that human beings *need*, however, not necessarily the love that they *want*. And this may perhaps be expressed not entirely inadequately as the compassionate outpouring of realistic affirmation. God is that reality which enables free human agency, even at the price of the divine self-effacement.

Church: Otherness and Difference

Let us wage war on totality; let us be witnesses to the unpresentable; let us activate the differences and save the honor of the name.
—Jean-François Lyotard

Here we return to the discussion first opened in the previous chapter, over the nature of a postmodern "faithful sociality," but modified to a degree by our examination of God-concepts appropriate to postmodernity. So, we may well ask how it is possible for faith communities today to be both faithful to their tradition and yet genuinely engaged in the wider human community. But "faithful to the tradition" means, among other things, faithful to an understanding of the divine as exercising a nonintrusive if not nonanthropocentric providence, and so stimulating the agency of human individuals and communities as vicars of the divine. In consequence, the dominant question that will arise here is whether sociality faithful to this understanding of God will lead to distinctive forms of involvement in the world. If the activity of Christian communities and individual Christians is simply indistinguishable from that of other communities and individuals, except that there is some purely internal motivation of faithfulness to a God who "cares" indiscriminately, then what would be the point of declaring one's sociality "faithful" at all? This question may indeed be one that the reader has posed, in slightly different form, in relation to the discussion of divine providence above. If my or our fortunes are not in effect "judged" by God and suitably rewarded, then what distinguishes believing in God from not believing in God, and if there is no difference, why bother?

The question raised in this section of the chapter for fundamental theology is that of the mission of a community of faith in the postmodern world. Given the postmodern recognition, which seems to me inescapable, that the world exhibits an irreducible plurality of view-points, and the rejection of the belief that one's own position is both unrevisable and in every respect superior to all others, that mission cannot consist in engaging in pluralistic discourse with the intention of persuading others to one's own point of view. It must rather be an engagement with the intention of reaching consensus through conversation or argument—conversation in which something is at stake. Now it must not be imagined for an instant that such a notion of discourse envisages the interlocutors as entering a dialogue in which none of them has any convictions at all about the shape society ought to take, or the types of attitudes or values that human beings ought to try to embody. Quite the contrary. We all bring with us to the conversation the world that has made us the people we are, but if discourse is to proceed this world must form the background out of which we operate, rather than a foreground that we hope to lead others to embrace.

Religious traditions often have serious problems with such a consensus theory of truth. Christianity in particular is persuaded of the truth of its narrative of salvation, and its responsibility to proclaim the gospel to the four corners of the earth. It would certainly seem difficult to accommodate to this an open and open-ended, revisable discourse oriented to consensus with individuals and groups whose own narratives, secular or religious, have little or nothing in common with that of Christianity. Surely, the argument proceeds, a narrative tradition forms our background, but doesn't it also shape us as actors with a vision, and indicate actions that will work toward the realization of that vision? Doesn't Milbank have it right? Doesn't Christianity lead naturally to Christendom?

A clue to the way we might address this problem is afforded by identifying the church as the community of faith which is the locus of revelation, while recognizing that Christian theology leads ineluctably to the conclusion that the world, not the church, is the locus of redemption. The corollary of this, of course, is that while the church is within the world, the world is not within the church. Given this distinction, the question of mission comes down to identifying the responsibility of the "community of revelation" to the "community of redemption" (in these words, a distinction used many years ago by Juan-Luis Segundo[7]). But the insights of postmodernity identify the community of redemption (that is, the world) as a place of relative, revisable, pragmatic, provisional "ways of seeing what-is." Unless we are committed to seeing this characteristic of postmodernity as error or even sin, the mode of mission that stands some chance of reception must be carefully identified.

Trying some thirty years ago to express a respectful attention to the ways of seeing of non-Christian religious traditions, Juan-Luis Segundo drew attention to the Second Vatican Council's assertion that the Church considers "whatever good or truth" is found among nonbelievers to be a "preparation for the gospel."[8] By this he meant to indicate that the presence of genuine and deeply held human values in non-Christian religious traditions was important in its own right, and predisposed those traditions to an encounter with divine grace, whether mediated or not through Christian mission. I believe that we can carry the idea a little further, however, and see the same sensibility at work in the mien of the postmodern church. Love, as "the compassionate outpouring of realistic affirmation," is the face of mission in a world convinced of the errancy of absolutes. And, of course, realistic affirmation is only another way of identifying the attitudes that must be brought to the encounter with the other.

In order to investigate further the precise characteristics of a community devoted to "the compassionate outpouring of realistic affirmation," I would like to borrow the very traditional ecclesiological notion of the faith community as a priestly, prophetic, and royal people. These terms, especially the last, need some reworking in order to be easily applicable in the postmodern context. Their initial attractiveness lies in their clarifying the background self-understanding of the community, however, rather than dictating this or that particular substantive element in its mission. Furthermore, these terms suggest a way of countering the potential charge that a church which engages the world as openly and in as nonsubstantive a way as we have suggested, has relinquished too much of its specificity. While the narrative may not be upfront in the moment of mission, the self-understanding to which the narrative has led is there instead. Let me proceed, then, by addressing each of these three terms in turn, trying to reexpress it in terminology more congenial to our age. Finally in this section we shall have to ask what material practices within the faith community correspond to such self-understanding.

To call the Christian community of faith a priestly people is to claim for them some share in the priestly role of Christ, the great high priest. It has, then, nothing to do with the use of the term *priest* in Catholic traditions to designate ordained ministers of the Eucharist. It relates, rather, to the Christian understanding of the Messiah as the one in whom God is present in the world. In the Messiah is seen the human shape of God, in the Messiah God is present in a way in which genuine reciprocal relationships are possible, and in the fate of the Messiah is seen the human way with the divine. Moreover, the gospel call to discipleship suggests a patterning of the life of the faith-community along the same lines. It will be a vessel of the Spirit, but also always a fleshly, historical, and distinctly human presence of that Spirit. And it will be a community of the Spirit under the sign of the cross.

To call the church priestly today is to highlight its sense of itself as having a mission to the world, in which it must in some clear way communicate the love of God in Christ to and for the world. *Not* communicate *that* God loves the world, but love the world for God, so to speak. Not claim to be the only or privileged divine servant, but certainly to feel driven to be *a* divine servant, one whose mission, however, is to love rather than talk about love. Thus, in the terminology of recent pages, we might say that the priestly character of the faith community is evidenced in the strength of its "*compassionate outpouring* of realistic affirmation." The obverse of such overwhelming care and concern for the world is a self-emptying. Redemption is only possible through kenosis. But then, the mission of the church is to involve itself in the redemption of the world, not to lead the world to the recognition that the church is the instrument of salvation.

This understanding of the church's mission is entirely consistent with the picture we have drawn of the relation of the faith community to the postmodern world as a whole. Here is a church whose principal objective *ad extra* is not to tell a story, but to help awaken that which is not church (and sometimes that which is) to the interpenetration of the cosmos and the divine, and to quicken the particular sense of responsibility to this cosmos and this God that it behooves the consciousness of creation to express. The raison d'être of the faith community is consequently always to face outward. But it cannot realistically understand itself as the only avenue of the divine into human history, the only manifestation of the Spirit.

We can and should pursue a similar retrieval of the notions of the church as a prophetic and as a royal people. The first of these is much the easier of the two to handle. The prophet, after all, is the one who speaks the truth to the world, and accepts—if unwillingly—the price that must sometimes be paid for speaking the truth. The stress here should not be on some semimasochistic embrace of the prophetic, however; rather, it should be a matter of emphasizing the candid and open attempt to encounter the world that is not church in a fully truthful manner. What of course may not have been so apparent in past times, but in our more rhetorically and hermeneutically conscious age cannot be escaped, is the importance of reception. The truth is not there to be spoken as some defiant proclamation of what must seem "folly to the Gentiles," or as a requirement laid upon the faith community before the full number of the days of this earth can be accomplished. The truth is to be expressed, as far as lies within the strength of the church to accomplish it, in a manner in which it can be received as true. And once again, what this suggests is a discourse model of "communicative action" based upon a search for con- sensus *in which everything is open for discussion but no responsibility to speak truth is surrendered.* And so we might say that the prophetic voice of the priestly people emphasizes the "compassionate outpouring of *realistic* affirmation." Prophecy today, in other words, is not a matter of present- ing a substantive message to an uncomprehending multitude, but rather of demanding—through acting out—an uncompromising openness to the future revealed through unconstrained discourse.

"Royalty" is a distinctly premodern notion. Where they exist today, monarchs no longer act as tyrants or enlightened despots, and most cer- tainly not as moral exemplars. Consequently, the idea of the church as a "royal" people must be quite dramatically rephrased. In the parlance of today's church, the phrase that captures best what was intended by the traditional christological and ecclesiological symbol of kingship and royalty is that of "servant-leader." This describes the ideal of the Davidic monarchy of ancient Israel, and the life-patterns of Christ, the Messiah who would suffer and die. Thus, discipleship of Christ will show itself most clearly in ecclesial communities that exercise leadership through service.

The stress on a leadership of service is particularly valuable, when what we are trying to do is to understand how to negotiate a role for the Christian community in a radically pluralistic political, cultural, and religious world. Structurally, I suppose, this suggests something like the early Jesuit approach to missionary activity in the ancient civilizations of the East. So Matteo Ricci became a Mandarin, Roberto da Nobili donned monk's robes and built an ashram, and the Jesuits of Nepal to this day run a high school and refrain entirely from proselytism. In traditional theological understanding, it makes sense as an attempt to cooperate with those cultural and religious impulses that Paul would have recognized as "a preparation for the gospel." But it also nicely captures the task of the church in the postmodern world: to meet the world which is not church where it is, on humble terms of equality, and to link arms in what may turn out to be a *very* long-term commitment to building a sustainable and worthwhile future for the world. Might we not say, then, that the servant-leader community meets the world in a posture of the "compassionate outpouring of realistic *affirmation*"?

We have seen in these few pages a sketch of a foundational ecclesiology for a Christian faith community encountering postmodernity. It must, we have seen, be deeply involved in its world, engaged in collaborative efforts toward the amelioration and elimination of problems, and confidently oriented toward a radically open future. But what do such theoretical claims mean for the material practices of the church? Present ecclesial structures are set up looking inward, for the most part, to the life of the faith community. Where mission and evangelism are stressed, they are promoted as ways of bringing more people into this essentially inward-looking community. The "corporal works of mercy," in which so many faith communities distinguish themselves, are almost always seen as subordinate to the "central" ministry of sacrament or word.

The present ecclesiological picture reverses the relationship of outreach and "inreach." The worship of the church, its sacramental life, as Juan-Luis Segundo suggested twenty-five years ago, is subordinate to and instrumental to the central work of the church, which is to minister to the needs of the world. Thus, as I have maintained elsewhere, and meaning no disrespect, the traditional ordained ministries of both Protestant and Catholic traditions are essentially—as ministers—support staff in the work of the church. That work is to be conducted by all the baptized in virtue of their baptism, but for the most part and perhaps by particular charism, by the "laity"—for want of a better word. At the present time, of course, this relationship is nowhere a living reality within the Christian community.

Among those forms of faithful sociality that we and others have singled out as distinctively postmodern, we find a number in which the lay/ordained distinction has been radically rethought. Of course, in some radical feminist Christian groupings the notion of "ordination" itself is suspect. In Rosemary Radford Ruether's "Womenchurch," for example, there are no ordained. All minister to one another. But for the most part, communities espousing some form of liberation theology have made the transition to the prominence of lay leadership. In the early church, to be an apostle was to be in the front line of interaction with nonchurch, often in polemical and sometimes in particularly hazardous situations. Over the centuries, the "successors of the apostles" (the bishops) in particular, and ordained ministers in general, have in many cultures come to be the least likely people to be found on the front lines where the church meets the world. Their roles, often for very good reasons, have now for a long time been understood predominantly in terms of the maintenance and presidency of the worshiping community of believers. But there is no self-evident reason why the *internal* leadership of the church should be identical to the external. Traditional theology in the Catholic tradition has long recognized this, in arguing that the work of the laity is in teaching by example, living in the world, while the clergy are taken up with the sacramental life of the church. But, of course, this in the traditional model must be understood in the context of a radical subordination of the external work of the church (conducted by the laity) to the sacramental life. When the latter is made instrumental to the former, when salvation is seen to require participation in the struggle for liberation, traditionalists will not follow.

Christ: The Personhood of God

We are dealing with the absolute God as he turned to us in the concrete uniqueness of Jesus Christ, so that this God really becomes the most concrete absolute.

—Karl Rahner

In our constructive attempt at postmodern apologetics, we have articulated a notion of the postmodern God at work in the background consciousness of Christians in the world, and an idea of the Christian community as inheritors of a tradition that strengthens them to do something other than talk about the tradition itself. We need finally to try to understand the way in which Christ plays a part in the background awareness of Christians. This way of expressing it even sounds odd. Isn't it the case, after all, that Christianity is christocentric, and don't Christians see Christ as the one, unique savior of the world, sent by God his Father? Would it not be treason, then, to leave this Christ languishing in our background awareness? Don't we have to "preach Christ, and him crucified"?

If you have come this far with me, you will know that my postmodern fundamental thelogy is not going to preach Christ in anything like a traditional sense. Like belief in God, however, belief in Christ has to make a difference if it is to be accounted real at all. So it must be possible for us to talk about the role of Christ in the Christian narrative making the Christian encounter with what is not church substantially different from the encounter with the world experienced by a nonchristocentric religious tradition. Indeed, we can go further and claim that while Christ will not be in the foreground of Christian mission in the postmodern world, Christ will be the distinctive element "behind" Christians engaged in this task.

It is at this point that we need to return to our considerations of the problem of anthropocentrism earlier in this chapter. We noted there that while God's providence must be understood as a care for the whole, the mode in which the care is offered to different elements in creation will be tailored to the way in which these different elements can receive providential care. Human beings are conscious, reflective agents who persistently incline to understand the world, and even God's providence, in a thoroughly anthropocentric way. From God's angle, so to speak, God has to deal with creatures who can both know and misunderstand divine providence at one and the same time. The problem for God is to negotiate how to enrich the knowledge and erase the misunderstanding. The opportunity for God, to pursue this thoroughly anthropomorphic metaphor, is that God has made human beings teachable.

If human beings are both free and teachable, then the message of which they can become conscious, about the nature of God and God's relationship with the world, must be presented in a way that does not involve God's intervention. God is the wholly other, beyond human apprehension, and even if that were not the case, then the clear self-communication of God would have to compromise human freedom. Christ, then, is the other of God, through whom the truth about God and the world is presented to human beings in a noncoercive way, all too open to misunderstanding and failure. Thus, in the death of Christ on the cross one sees at once the destructive freedom of the human race in face of the divine, and a representation of exactly the message of the divine for the human, namely, that human selflessness, self-abnegation, and the embrace of failure and death are the way in which the world can be saved from and for itself.

The role of Christ in the background consciousness of the Christian and the whole faith community is then at one and the same time to confirm that the silent and distant God speaks in the world in Christ as the other of God, and speaks a sign of contradiction that says, quite literally, that human life must be lived on the way of the cross. This, by the way, is where I would part company with Jean-Luc Marion. Christ the icon of God is *not* transparent at all, but deeply and ineradicably colored by historical circumstance and profoundly reflective of the tragedy of being human in a nonanthropocentric universe. The drama of Christ the human God, like that of all human beings, is one of learning self-surrender. God only knows this in Christ. And thus the icon adds something to that which is shining through it.

This christological moment in fundamental theology changes our perception of the background awareness of the Christian. Whereas the postmodern appropriation of a God-concept is a limitation upon the believer, the understanding of Christ at work here casts aside those limits. God's providential care is a care of the whole, but Christ is the mode of care that God has suited to human receptivity, and this Christ reinforces in his life and death the strength of human responsibility and courage even within the constraints of a nonanthropocentric universe. The postmodern Christian must come to terms, as we have argued, with the notion that the providential care of God is extended without favoritism to the whole creation on the same terms. But "in Christ" the Christian is able to view the entire economy of salvation through the divine focused in the human because this is the only way in which the human can receive this nonanthropocentric teaching. Thus, "following Christ" *is* salvation and not merely *the way to* salvation, because the following of this "divine other" is human acquiescence to our place in the divine scheme of things.

We may carry a little further this thought about the christological background of the Christian's engagement with the world by pressing the concept of Christ as the other of God. Again, comparison with Marion may be instructive. In Marion, Christ is the icon of God, the transparent symbol through which God reaches out as pure gift to the human race. While I think Marion is substantially correct in his phenomenology of idol and icon, and in his preference for the latter, I have already suggested a limitation or two that pertain to the transparency of the icon. The concrete historical particularity of Christ is an important element in the reception of God on the part of Christians. The wholly transparent would be a conduit only for the *mysterium tremendum et fascinans* (awesome and fascinating mystery) at best, and at worst for a fearful and uncomprehending obeisance before the wholly other. The anthropomorphism and even a measure of the anthropocentrism that the figure of Christ encourages are the price of reception.

To suggest that Christ may perhaps best be understood, at least in our times, as the other of God, requires a little explanation. Christ's historical particularity, of course, suggests certain polarities between Christ and God—so, human and divine, historical and eternal, omniscient and subject to human limitations, and so on. But the notion of the other is more than that. The other is the one who is not me, yet in whom I see myself reflected. The gaze of the other, indeed, is that which confirms me in my personhood. I am dependent on the other, as the other is dependent on me. In the relationship between the creator God and the Christ who proceeds from the creator, the other whom the creator constitutes as other is the initially dependent one, upon whom the creator eventually comes to depend. The procession of the Christ is the kenosis of the creator. God the creator is affirmed as creator by that other of God which is the only way through which the human misunderstanding of providential care can become pure knowledge of providential care.

In chapter 2, the question of Christology was addressed through the issue of the theology of religions. What is the relationship, we implied, between the particularity of Christian salvation in Christ and the claims that God's salvific will is toward universal salvation? While we considered there the various options that are bruited about, and particularly the various forms of pluralism which struggle to express the postmodern conviction that there are other ways to salvation, we also sat on the fence. At this point, armed with our understanding of Christ as the other of God, as the nontransparent historically particular presence of God, we can finally address this central concern about "other religions."

The particularity of Christ in the Christian narrative, we have argued, is usefully understood today under the rubric of "the other of God." In Christ, that God who is yet not God, that not-God who is yet divine, the Christian faith community can receive the profoundly nonanthropocentric message that God's providential care for creation does not imply any special preference for human beings. At the same time, the very special way in which this message is presented, the only mode in which reception can occur for human beings, is indicative of God's inclusion of human beings within the domain of divine providence. Salvation, to quote Nietzsche, is found in "being faithful to the earth," through which we find our place in the divine scheme of things. And to follow Zarathustra just a little further, while this involves recognition of our inescapable mortality, it is no simple affirmation of mere materiality.

The mission of the Christian faith community is then to live in this world in ways that witness to the truth of God's relationship to creation in general and to human beings in particular. For this reason if for no other, the Christian community should be concerned less with putting Christ, and still less itself, in the foreground and more with proclaiming the truth about God revealed through Christ. This "truth about God" is not itself specific to the Christian tradition, however. On the contrary, the recognition that the divine stands in a supportive and compassionate relationship to the whole of creation is an insight com-

mon to Western religious traditions. Moreover, this insight is susceptible of expression in language more compatible with Eastern thought:
the essential mystery of life is not the mere sum total of what-is, and
salvation lies in making this realization truly one's own. What is distinctive about Christianity remains within Christianity and in no way
challenges or represents itself as superior to other religious traditions,
namely, the belief that in Christ God has spoken in a way that human
beings can receive the word. Moreover, the particularity lies in the messenger, not in the message, though the character of the messenger is
crucial in the possibility of reception. The human face of the divine, in
all its particularity, historicality, and concreteness, shines through it.

There are, in the end, two and only two ways in which Christian churches can engage with the postmodern world. They can try to convert it to
Christ, or they can not. The former, more evangelical position admits of
a variety of levels of subtlety in its proclamation of the gospel. It can be
triumphalistic, stentorian, and abrasive at one extreme; at the other, it
can be gentle, compassionate, and low-key. But whether at either end of
the spectrum or somewhere in the middle, the procedural understanding
of Christian mission is identical. The Christian economy of redemption
is the ground, the hermeneutical grid on which the church and the
nonchurch must meet. The latter position suspends evangelism in the
name of what it considers a more fundamental dimension of its mission,
namely, sacramental presence. Whether the salt of the earth, the leaven in
the mass, the beacon on the hill, or the quasi-mystical and almost gnostic
"community of revelation," its relationship to the non-Christian world is
one whose tactics *and* strategy differ markedly from the first position.
While related to the world, it does not seek to absorb it.

While the evangelical perspective is perhaps most at home in the premodern world, and the liberal outlook is quintessentially modern, both
have their postmodern forms. Both, that is, recognize the pluriformity
of the postmodern world. But in keeping with their respective estima-
tions of the world beyond the church, the former encounters the otherness of postmodernity as challenge to be overcome, while the latter finds
it a fact to celebrate. Thus, while the one operates on the imperatives of
conversion to Christ, the other is content with the solidarity of mutual

respect. Evangelization is the remedy for complacency and lukewarmness; solidarity is the cure for triumphalism and self-righteousness.

In the final analysis, neither alternative is wholly right, and neither is entirely erroneous. The perduring weakness of liberalism is its tendency toward relativism, and the evangelical tradition insists upon the specificity and uniqueness of the Christian gospel. The failing of evangelicalism, on the contrary, lies in its tendency to equate uniqueness with preeminence. Here the liberal variety of postmodern religion is valuable, insisting that uniqueness need not be equivalent to some abstract notion of superiority or privileged truth. So, I can be wholly committed to my own religious tradition and fully persuaded of its account of reality, while feeling neither threatened by nor needing to overcome alternative accounts of reality.

Postmodernity has a lesson for Christianity, and the religious tradition can enlighten the postmodern sensibility. In the postmodern world, we have seen throughout this short text and we know from our experience, there are many alternative versions of reality, many different ways of being in the world, and we have noted the tolerance of postmodernity for this plethora of possibilities. This, I believe, is important to Christian theology, with its age-old tendency to reduce the other to "that which needs to be explained in terms of the central hermeneutic significance of Christ." But in a similar way, Christian faith in the postmodern world is a salutary challenge to postmodernity's insouciance, that among the great variety of options, *it is important to choose one.* Now, as I have also hinted immediately above, the one who is committed to Christianity needs to stop there and not proceed to extravagant claims about the exclusive superiority of the tradition. As Christians, we can and should engage the world in all its variety of plumage, and rejoice in its multifarious ways of seeing. We should not try to convert it to what it is not. But we should simultaneously rejoice in who we are. We are what we are, in a posture of deep commitment, and "they" are what they are. And this is just perfectly fine.

Notes

Preface

1. Some, of course, are more persuasive and thought-provoking than others. Among the more important are David Harvey, Ihab Hassan, Andreas Huyssen, Fredric Jameson, Jean-François Lyotard, and Richard Rorty (see notes for information on specific works).

2. Jean-François Lyotard, *The Postmodern Condition: A Report on Knowledge* (Minneapolis: University of Minnesota Press, 1984); idem, *The Differend: phrases in dispute* (Minneapolis: University of Minnesota Press, 1988); Fredric Jameson, *Postmodernism, or, The Cultural Logic of Late Capitalism* (Durham, N.C.: Duke University Press, 1991); Terry Eagleton, *The Significance of Theory* and *The Ideology of the Aesthetic* (both Oxford: Oxford University Press, 1989); idem, "Awakening from Modernity," in the *Times Literary Supplement*, 20 February 1987; and Richard Bernstein, ed., *Habermas and Modernity* (Oxford: Oxford University Press, 1985).

3. In the introduction to *The Anti-Aesthetic: Essays on Postmodern Culture* (Port Townsend, Wash.: Bay Press, 1983).

4. "Mapping the Postmodern" in *Feminism/Postmodernism*, ed. Linda J. Nicholson (New York and London: Routledge, 1990), 234–77. This essay was published originally in *New German Critique* 33 (1984): 5–52. See also *After the Great Divide: Modernism, Mass Culture, Postmodernism* (Bloomington: Indiana University Press, 1986).

5. *The Condition of Postmodernity: An Enquiry into the Origins of Cultural Change* (Oxford: Basil Blackwell, 1989).

6. *Against Postmodernism: A Marxist Critique* (New York: St. Martin's Press, 1990).

7. *Political Theory and Postmodernism* (Cambridge: Cambridge University Press, 1991).

8. Something of this kind of analysis of postmodernism has been attempted by Fredric Jameson in "The Politics of Theory: Ideological Positions in the Postmodernism Debate," *New German Critique* 33 (1984): 53–65. The article is reprinted and slightly expanded as chap. 2 of Jameson's 1991 book, *Postmodernism*, 55–66.

9. It is the organizing principle, if such is possible, of a recent collection of essays devoted to showing that postmodernity has no organizing principle or set of salient characteristics. See Ingeborg Hoesterey, ed., *Zeitgeist in Babel: The Post-Modernist Controversy* (Bloomington: Indiana University Press, 1991).

1. Postmodernity

1. Many examples are available. Fredric Jameson, for example, has written at length about the postmodern intent of the Westin Bonaventure in downtown Los Angeles. Here I have in mind the Marriott in Atlanta's downtown, but the point could be made today in almost any major city in North America, Western Europe, or the Far East.

2. A phrase, indeed, used by Marshall Berman in the title of a book about modernity.

3. Wolfe's Sherman McCoy is of course the central figure in the immensely successful *Bonfire of the Vanities* (New York: Farrar, Straus and Giroux, 1987). John Self is the protagonist of what is actually a rather more persuasive picture of the same world, and a rather more self-consciously postmodern novel, Martin Amis's *Money: A Suicide Note* (London: Jonathan Cape, 1984). In fact, Amis's entire corpus of fiction to date—significant for a writer who is still quite young—presents one of the clearest pictures of the darker side of postmodernity. Those interested in pursuing postmodernity through literature could also profitably attend to the writings of Jay McInerney, Alasdair Gray, and Douglas Coupland.

4. These the reader might perceive as cheap shots, and certainly it is more the public personae of these individuals that make them representative of the category, rather than—necessarily—their private selves. On the other hand, it is perhaps the suspicion that they have collapsed the latter into the former that puts them high on the list. An even better example is the Australian comedian Barry Humphrey's creation, Dame Edna Everedge, a frightening and alluring individual who is ambiguously related to her creator, sexually ambiguous, and who has absolutely no self. She is real only in the reflection of the many celebrities with whom she surrounds herself. Why these real celebrities are prepared to play out this fantasy with a quite unreal person is, of course, an entirely different question.

5. Victor Frankl, *Man's Search for Meaning* (New York: Pocket Books, 1959).

6. *Death by Bread Alone: Texts and Reflections on Religious Experience* (Philadelphia: Fortress Press, 1978), 8.

7. This generally accepted and usually noncontroversial estimation of the Enlightenment has recently been cogently challenged by Louis Dupré in *Passage to Modernity: An Essay in the Hermeneutics of Nature and Culture* (New Haven/London: Yale University Press, 1993). Dupré argues that the nominalist disintegration of the classical worldview is the real originator of modernity.

8. Max Horkheimer and Theodor Adorno, *Dialectic of Enlightenment* (New York: Herder & Herder, 1972).

9. Kant's essay was written in 1784. See *Foundations of the Metaphysics of Morals and What Is Enlightenment?*, trans. with an introduction by Lewis White Beck (Indianapolis: Bobbs-Merrill, 1959), 85–92.

10. Michel Foucault, "The Art of Telling the Truth," in *Critique and Power: Recasting the Foucault–Habermas Debate,* ed. Michael Kelly (Cambridge, Mass.: MIT Press, 1994), 140.

11. *The Foucault Reader,* ed. Paul Rabinow (New York: Pantheon, 1984) 41–42.

12. "The Art of Telling the Truth," 147–48.

13. See Habermas's reflective essay written in memory of Foucault, "Taking Aim at the Heart of the Present," in *Critique and Power*, 149–54.

14. Jürgen Habermas, *The Philosophical Discourse of Modernity: Twelve Lectures* (Cambridge, Mass.: MIT Press, 1987), 33.

15. Ibid., 20.

16. I take these terms from Charles Taylor's monumental survey of modern thought, *Sources of the Self: The Making of the Modern Identity* (Cambridge, Mass.: Harvard University Press, 1989). Those without the time, patience, or background knowledge for this work can get the gist of the argument from the same author's *The Ethics of Authenticity* (Cambridge, Mass.: Harvard University Press, 1991).

17. Richard Rorty, *Philosophy and the Mirror of Nature* (Princeton: Princeton University Press, 1979); and idem, *Contingency, Irony and Solidarity* (Cambridge and New York: Cambridge University Press, 1989).

18. Michael Walzer's phrase in "The Politics of Michel Foucault," published in *Foucault: A Critical Reader*, ed. David Couzens Hoy (Oxford and New York: Basil Blackwell, 1986), 51–68. This citation is from p. 63.

19. Habermas, *Philosophical Discourse of Modernity*, 57.

20. See above all Habermas's *The Theory of Communicative Action*. Volume One: *Reason and the Rationalization of Society;* Volume Two: *Lifeworld and System* (Boston: Beacon Press, 1984, 1988) and *Justification and Application: Remarks on Discourse Ethics* (Cambridge, Mass.: MIT Press, 1993).

21. Taylor, *Sources of the Self*, 514–15.

22. Sir Isaiah Berlin, writing of Herder and Vico, is careful to distinguish their "pluralism" from the "relativism" of which they are so often accused. Vico and Herder, he adds, are oblivious of "the mazes of false consciousness." See "Alleged Relativism in Eighteenth-Century Thought," in Berlin's collection of essays, *The Crooked Timber of Humanity: Essays in the History of Ideas* (New York: Knopf, 1991), 70–90. This quotation is found on p. 85.

23. Richard Rorty, ed., *The Linguistic Turn: Recent Essays in Philosophical Method* (Chicago: University of Chicago Press, 1967); see also *Current Issues in Theology 2: The Linguistic Turn*, ed. Michael Scanlon (Macon, Ga.: Mercer University Press, 1987).

24. Michel Foucault, *Discipline and Punish: The Birth of the Prison* (New York: Vintage Books, 1979).

25. Ibid., 30.

26. Ibid., 222.

27. Ibid., 29–30.

28. Michel Foucault, *The Order of Things: An Archaeology of the Human Sciences* (New York: Pantheon Books, 1970).

29. Rorty, *Contingency, Irony and Solidarity*, 61. On p. xv Rorty explains the somewhat unusual senses in which he uses the two terms. Liberals "are the people who think that cruelty is the worst thing that we do," while an ironist is "the sort of person who faces up to the contingency of his or her own most central beliefs and desires."

30. An outstanding exception to this is Allan Megill, *Prophets of Extremity: Nietzsche, Heidegger, Foucault, Derrida* (Berkeley: University of California Press, 1985).

31. Martin Heidegger, *Existence and Being* (South Bend, Ind.: Gateway Editions, 1949), 325–61.

32. Ibid., 339.

33. Martin Heidegger, *The Question concerning Technology and Other Essays* (New York: Harper & Row, 1977), 139–41.

34. John Dewey's phrase, adopted by Rorty. But Rorty has abandoned even that limited essentialism for "truth is not the sort of thing one should expect to have a philosophically interesting theory about" (*Consequences of Pragmatism: Essays, 1972–1980* [Minneapolis: University of Minnesota Press, 1982], xiii).

35. Foucault, of course, above all.

36. Rorty, *Contingency, Irony and Solidarity,* xiv.

37. This view is associated most of all with Alasdair MacIntyre.

38. Jürgen Habermas, *Justification and Application: Remarks on Discourse Ethics* (Cambridge, Mass.: MIT Press, 1993), and Seyla Benhabib, *Critique, Norm and Utopia: A Study of the Foundations of Critical Theory* (New York: Columbia University Press, 1986).

39. For example and perhaps above all, Jeffrey Stout's *Ethics after Babel: The Languages of Morals and Their Discontents* (Boston: Beacon Press, 1988).

40. Ibid., 214.

41. David R. Hiley, *Philosophy in Question: Essays on a Pyrrhonian Theme* (Chicago and London: University of Chicago Press, 1988), 105–14.

42. For an excellent discussion of Foucault's relationship to Kant on this matter, see James Miller's *The Passion of Michel Foucault* (New York: Simon & Schuster, 1993), 332–34.

43. Another book in the *Guides to Theological Inquiry* series examines in depth the whole question of nonfoundationalism and its relevance for religious thought. See John E. Thiel, *Nonfoundationalism* (Minneapolis: Fortress Press, 1994). Thiel would not see fideism and (religious) nonfoundationalism as synonymous. One who would probably be more sympathetic to such an understanding is James M. Gustafson, though the term he prefers to fideism is "sectarian tribalism." See "The Sectarian Temptation: Reflections on Theology, the Church and the University," in *Proceedings of the Catholic Theological Society of America* 40 (1985): 83–94.

44. Alasdair McIntyre, *After Virtue: A Study in Moral Theory* (Notre Dame, Ind.: University of Notre Dame Press, 1981).

45. Ibid., 175–78.

46. Ibid., 206.

47. The political problem of otherness in postmodern discourse is particularly well handled by Stephen K. White in *Political Theory and Postmodernism* (Cambridge: Cambridge University Press, 1991).

48. Ibid., 16.

49. In Jean-François Lyotard, *The Postmodern Condition: A Report on Knowledge* (Minneapolis: University of Minnesota Press, 1984). This "increasing incredulity towards metanarratives" is identified by Stephen White as one of four interrelated phenomena which together characterize postmodernity. The other three are "the growing

awareness of new problems wrought by societal rationalization," "the explosion of new informational technologies," and "the emergence of new social movements" (*Political Theory*, 4).

50. Hal Foster, *The Anti-Aesthetic: Essays on Postmodern Culture* (Port Townsend, Wash.: Bay Press, 1983), xii.

51. Nostalgic postmodernism seems to correspond to Hal Foster's second type, a "postmodernism of reaction" that rejects modernism and embraces the status quo. This is in its turn is what Habermas has in mind in his depiction of postmodernism as neoconservatism (see "Modernity—An Incomplete Project," in *The Anti-Aesthetic*, 3–15).

52. Jean-Paul Sartre, *Existentialism and Humanism* (London: Methuen, 1948), 39.

53. See n.14 above.

54. Taylor, *Sources of the Self*, 16.

55. Ibid., 23.

56. The religious issues raised by Taylor's work are explored in James J. Buckley, "A Return to the Subject: The Theological Significance of Charles Taylor's Sources of the Self," *The Thomist* 55/3 (July 1991): 497–509.

57. Taylor, *Sources of the Self*, 513.

58. *Theology and Social Theory: Beyond Secular Reason* (Oxford and Cambridge, Mass.: Basil Blackwell, 1990), 434.

59. The bibliography of postmodern science is vast. Among the religiously oriented works that enter into dialogue with or represent postmodern scientific thinking are the following: Paul Davies, *The Mind of God: The Scientific Basis for a Rational World* (New York: Simon & Schuster, 1992); Philip Hefner, *The Human Factor: Evolution, Culture and Religion*, Theology and the Sciences (Minneapolis: Fortress Press, 1993); Arthur Peacocke, *God and the New Biology* (London: J. M. Dent, 1986); and Stephen Toulmin, *The Return to Cosmology: Postmodern Science and the Theology of Nature* (Berkeley: University of California Press, 1982).

60. This point is well made by Sallie McFague in her essay "Cosmology and Christianity: Implications of the Common Creation Story for Theology," in *Theology at the End of Modernity*, ed. Sheila Davaney (Philadelphia: TPI, 1991), 19–40, esp. 21–25.

2. Religion

1. See John Thiel, *Imagination and Authority: Theological Authorship in the Modern Tradition* (Minneapolis: Fortress Press, 1991), for a careful historical exposition of the relationship between creativity and the theological task.

2. Above all, the writings of Mark C. Taylor and Thomas Altizer.

3. See Altizer's latest work, *Genesis and Apocalypse: A Theological Voyage toward Authentic Christianity* (Louisville: Westminster John Knox Press, 1990).

4. Mark C. Taylor, *Altarity* (Chicago: University of Chicago Press, 1987), xxii.

5. Leonardo Boff's *Ecology and Liberation* (Maryknoll, N.Y.: Orbis Books, 1995) is very helpful on this point, pressing liberation theology beyond its anthropocentric vision, while at the same time naming the modernity/capitalism axis as the prime locus

and instigator of evil. On the other hand, Boff looks to a renewed modernism rather than a postmodernism to intercede on behalf of the world.

6. Helmut Peukert, *Science, Action, Fundamental Theology: Toward a Theology of Communicative Action* (Cambridge, Mass.: MIT Press, 1984), 239.

7. Gordon Kaufman, *In Face of Mystery: A Constructive Theology* (Cambridge, Mass.: Harvard University Press, 1993), 79.

8. See especially "The Uneasy Alliance Reconceived: Catholic Theological Method, Modernity and Postmodernity," *Theological Studies* 50 (1989): 548–70; "Theology and the Many Faces of Postmodernity," *Theology Today* 51 (April 1994): 104–14; and "Literary Theory and Return of the Forms for Naming and Thinking God in Theology," *Journal of Religion* 74 (July 1994): 302–19.

9. *The Body of God: An Ecological Theology* (Minneapolis: Fortress Press, 1993).

10. Peter C. Hodgson, *Winds of the Spirit: A Constructive Christian Theology* (Louisville: Westminster John Knox Press, 1994), 4.

11. For a fine text focused on God's acting, but one that appeared too late for serious consideration in this book, see Edward Farley's *Divine Empathy: A Theology of God* (Minneapolis: Fortress Press, 1996).

12. James Gustafson, *Ethics from a Theocentric Perspective*. Vol. 1: *Theology and Ethics* (Cleveland: United Church Press, 1983), 237.

13. Ibid., 239.

14. Ibid., 249.

15. Ibid., 264.

16. Ibid., 164.

17. Ibid., 247.

18. For a helpful review of some of Gustafson's most serious critics, see David Schenck, "Reflections on Responses to Gustafson's *Ethics from a Theocentric Perspective,*" *Journal of Religion* 14/1 (Spring 1986): 72–85. For the particular charge of Stoicism, see Stephen Toulmin's essay, "Nature and Nature's God," *Journal of Religious Ethics* 13/1 (Spring 1985): 37–52. Incidentally, Gustafson has expressed approval of much of Toulmin's critique.

19. Gustafson, *Ethics from a Theocentric Perspective*, vol. 1, 113.

20. Ibid., 112.

21. Elie Wiesel, *Night* (New York: Avon, 1969), 67.

22. While many of Kaufman's books have carried this project forward, I shall concentrate entirely on his most complete exposition, *In Face of Mystery: A Constructive Theology*.

23. Ibid., 43.

24. Ibid., 322.

25. Ibid., 326.

26. Ibid., 264–97.

27. Ibid., 326.

28. Above all in her latest book, *The Body of God: An Ecological Theology*.

29. Ibid., 135.

30. Ibid., 144.

31. Ibid., 146.

32. In *Winds of the Spirit: A Constructive Christian Theology.*

33. Ibid., 148.

34. Ibid., 157.

35. While there is much writing on the base communities, the best book on ecclesiological implications is undoubtedly Leonardo Boff's *Ecclesiogenesis: The Base Communities Reinvent the Church* (Maryknoll, N.Y.: Orbis Books, 1986).

36. In this connection the work of Michel de Certeau and Mikhail Bakhtin are important, both in their different ways of recognizing the importance of a theological "underclass." Bakhtin sees carnival as the subversive reversal of order, while de Certeau distinguishes between two types of symbolic change, the strategic (or official adjustment of symbols) and the tactical, the latter the free creative work of those not "in control." On these authors see Philip J. Chmielewski, "De Certeau, Tactics and Chaos: Interpretive Social Science and Inter-Cultural Missionary Encounter," *Église et Théologie* 25 (1994): 219–37. The connections between these insights and the contemporary ethical attention to practices is evident. Also related here is the work of Michael Warren on the "material conditions" of ecclesial life, in "The Local Church and Its Practice of the Gospel: The Materiality of Discipleship in a Catechesis of Liberation," *Worship* 67/5 (1992): 433–60. Finally, a recent book by Bernard J. Lee sketches out a lay interpretation of Catholic Christian identity, and of course in the Catholic tradition the laity are most assuredly the underside! See *The Future Church of 140 B.C.E.: A Hidden Revolution* (New York: Crossroad, 1995).

37. On this see especially Leonardo Boff, *Ecology and Liberation: A New Paradigm* (Maryknoll, N.Y.: Orbis Books, 1995), 93–130, and Ignacio Ellacuria, "Uncovering a Civilization of Capital, Discovering a Civilization of Work," in David Batstone, ed., *New Visions for the Americas: Religious Engagement and Social Transformation* (Minneapolis: Fortress Press, 1993), 72–82.

38. George Lindbeck, *The Nature of Doctrine* (Philadelphia: Westminster Press, 1984).

39. See "Ecumenism and the Future of Belief," *Una Sancta* 25/3 (1968): 3–17; "The Sectarian Future of the Church" in *The God Experience*, ed. Joseph P. Whelen (New York: Newman Press, 1971), 226–43; and especially "The Story-Shaped Church," in *Scriptural Authority and Narrative Interpretation*, ed. Garrett Green (Philadelphia: Fortress Press, 1987), 161–79.

40. For the postliberal ecclesiology of Hauerwas, see especially *A Community of Character: Toward a Constructive Christian Social Ethic* (Notre Dame, Ind.: University of Notre Dame Press, 1981), and "The Church as God's New Language," in Green, ed., *Scriptural Authority and Narrative Interpretation*, 179–98. The present quotation is from *A Community of Character*, 12.

41. Lindbeck, *The Nature of Doctrine*, 118.

42. "Church Discourse and Public Realm," in *Theology and Dialogue: Essays in Conversation with George Lindbeck*, ed. Bruce D. Marshall (Notre Dame, Ind.: University of Notre Dame Press, 1990), 7–33. This quotation is from p. 8.

43. Lindbeck, "The Story-Shaped Church," in Green, ed., *Scriptural Authority and Narrative Interpretation*, 175.

44. See "The Jordan, the Tiber and the Ganges: Three Kairological Moments of Christic Self-Consciousness," in *The Myth of Christian Uniqueness: Toward a Pluralistic Theology of Religions*, ed. John Hick and Paul F. Knitter (Maryknoll, N.Y.: Orbis Books, 1987), 89–116.

45. John Milbank, *Theology and Social Theory* (Cambridge, Mass.: Basil Blackwell, 1991).

46. Ibid., 388.

47. Ibid.

48. Ibid., 402.

49. Ibid., 411.

50. Ibid., 417.

51. John Milbank, "'Postmodern Critical Augustinianism': A Short *Summa* in Forty-Two Responses to Unasked Questions," *Modern Theology* 7/3 (April 1991): 225–37. This set of theses, published subsequent to the appearance of the book, is actually a very good place to begin trying to understand Milbank's argument, though like the book the "answers" begin with great clarity and end in near-impenetrability. The brief quotations here are from p. 227.

52. Ibid., 226.

53. Milbank, *Theology and Social Theory*, 140.

54. Ibid., 410.

55. Ibid., 417.

56. Especially *Contingency, Irony and Solidarity* (Cambridge and New York: Cambridge University Press, 1989).

57. In the two volumes of *The Theory of Communicative Action, Reason and the Rationalization of Society* and *Lifeworld and System* (Boston: Beacon Press, 1984, 1988).

58. Leonard Swidler, *Toward a Universal Theology of Religion* (Maryknoll, N.Y.: Orbis Books, 1987).

59. John Hick, "The Non-Absoluteness of Christianity," in Hick and Knitter, eds., *The Myth of Christian Uniqueness: Toward a Pluralistic Theology of Religions* (Maryknoll, N.Y.: Orbis Books, 1987), 16–36.

60. The best single source for this point of view is undoubtedly *Christian Uniqueness Reconsidered: The Myth of a Pluralistic Theology of Religions*, ed. Gavin D'Costa (Maryknoll, N.Y.: Orbis Books, 1990).

61. Hick and Knitter, eds., *The Myth of Christian Uniqueness*, viii.

62. D'Costa, *Christian Uniqueness Reconsidered*, x.

63. Here one might with profit read Kathryn Tanner's essay on the "plain sense" of the narrative. See Kathryn E. Tanner, "Theology and the Plain Sense," in Green, ed., *Scriptural Authority and Narrative Interpretation*, 59–78.

64. Panikkar, "The Jordan, the Tiber and the Ganges," in Hick and Knitter, *The Myth of Christian Uniqueness*, 109.

65. Langdon Gilkey, "Plurality and Its Theological Implications," in ibid., 37–50.

66. Ibid., 47.

67. Ibid., 49.

68. Panikkar, "The Jordan, the Tiber and the Ganges," in ibid., 103.

69. Ibid., 92.

70. Ibid.

71. D'Costa, "Christ, the Trinity and Religious Plurality," in D'Costa, ed., *Christian Uniqueness Reconsidered*, 18–19.

72. John Cobb, "Beyond 'Pluralism,'" in ibid., 92.

73. J. A. DiNoia, "Pluralist Theology of Religions: Pluralistic or Non-Pluralistic?" in ibid., 133.

74. Gordon Kaufman, "Religious Diversity, Historical Consciousness and Christian Theology," in ibid., 3–15.

75. Ibid., 4–5.

76. Gilkey, "Plurality and Its Theological Implications," in Hick and Knitter, 44.

77. *The Classic* (Cambridge, Mass.: Harvard University Press, 1983), 138–41.

3. A Postmodern Apologetics

1. While I would prefer to use the term *foundational* here, the earlier discussion of foundationalism and nonfoundationalism in theology could lead to misunderstandings, and so I shall refer to this form of theology by the term *fundamental*.

2. Only in January 1996 was it discovered that the previous assumption that the universe contained some ten billion galaxies is probably wildly wrong. The true number is closer to fifty billion. When we also recall that our own galaxy contains between fifty and one hundred billion stars, who would care to argue that the chances of intelligent life elsewhere in the universe are not reasonably good?

3. Jean-Luc Marion, *God without Being: Hors-Texte* (Chicago: University of Chicago Press, 1991).

4. See "On Reading the Scriptures Theologically," in *Theology in Dialogue: Essays in Conversation with George Lindbeck*, ed. Bruce D. Marshall (Notre Dame, Ind.: University of Notre Dame Press, 1990), 35–65, and esp. 51–55.

5. There is, of course, an enormous amount of literature about the meaning of the book of Job. I cannot rehearse it here. Let is suffice to say that my own position on the meaning of the text, while it is not undisputed, has many authoritative voices on its side. Two helpful locations of thoughtful work on Job are in the introduction to Stephen Mitchell's translation, *The Book of Job* (San Francisco: North Point Press, 1987), and, somewhat more surprisingly, in William Safire's *The First Dissident: The Book of Job in Today's Politics* (New York: Random House, 1992).

6. A similar point is made by Jean-Luc Marion in his phenomenology of God as giving, or in relation to human beings as "being-given par excellence" ("Metaphysics and Phenomenology: A Relief for Theology," *Critical Inquiry* 20 [Summer 1994]: 572–91; see p. 588). This unreserved giving so saturates reality that God cannot be present as an object; thus the presence of God may seem very like absence. If the God of Job's whirlwind were acquainted with Edmund Husserl, just such a formulation might meet with considerable approval.

7. In Juan-Luis Segundo, *The Community Called Church* (Maryknoll, N.Y.: Orbis Books, 1973).

8. Second Vatican Council, *Lumen Gentium*, para. 16.

Glossary

anthropocentrism: the tendency toward or practice of understanding reality as solely or primarily instrumental to human needs and purposes.

anthropomorphism: the representation of any nonhuman reality or being as possessing characteristics or attributes particular to human beings.

apologetics: a division of theology that is concerned to defend and explain the reasonableness of Christian faith.

apophatic: Religious language or accounts of mystical experience in which the holy is approached by way of stressing otherness and incomprehensibility; the way of negation.

bricolage: a nonsystematic approach to understanding, which proceeds by the piecemeal gathering and juxtaposition of apparently disconnected items. "Collage" or the "quilt" approach to truth.

deconstruction: see "poststructuralism."

demythologization: the term developed by Rudolf Bultmann to describe the process of eliminating elements of ancient worldviews in scripture and religious language, so that the core anthropological truths can emerge.

dialectic: a philosophical method in which understanding occurs through holding apparently opposed principles or truths in tension, so that a higher viewpoint in which both are retained will emerge. So, for example, attention both to cross and resurrection are necessary in a Christian theology of redemption if the full richness of the doctrine is to be maintained.

epistemology: the branch of philosophy that deals with how we can know that we know, with the way in which knowledge occurs, and with the limits of our knowledge.

eschatology: theological subject matter concerned with the consummation of all things at the end of time or, more narrowly, with beliefs about individual and communal destiny.

fideism: the belief that religious truth is accessible only through faith, not through reason.

foundationalism: the philosophical and theological conviction that there are beliefs or experiences that are in themselves beyond doubt, and upon which systems of belief and understanding can therefore be constructed with certainty.

fusion of horizons: a term coined by the philosopher Hans-Georg Gadamer to describe the way in which the world of the text and the world of the reader may somehow be seen to overlap, through their common participation in a living tradition.

genealogy: in contemporary philosophy and historiography, this refers to a method of examining data that traces paths and linkages without imposing any explanatory framework upon them.

hermeneutics: the study of methods and principles of interpretation, with particular reference in theology to the question of the mediation of truth through texts.

historicism: a critical approach that insists on the inevitability of the historical conditioning of all statements, formulations, perceptions.

metaphysics: the branch of philosophy that examines ultimate questions, the nature of things, and the meaning of existence.

mysticism: direct experience of or contact with the holy, the sacred, or the numinous.

neoorthodoxy: a theological school, usually associated with the work of Karl Barth, which challenged liberal and modernist theological approaches, insisting on a biblical faith and on the centrality of the doctrine of justification by grace through faith in Christ.

neopragmatism: the new wave in predominantly American philosophy, owing much to the earlier American pragmatism of John Dewey, William James, and Charles Sanders Peirce, in which thinking guides action and truth is a matter of functional utility. Particularly associated with the work of Richard Rorty.

nominalism: the philosophical view that no essences or abstract universals exist in reality.

nonfoundationalism: a philosophical approach critical of any assumption that there are certain and stable foundations for knowing, upon which other claims can be built.

ontology: the branch of philosophy that studies "being" itself.

panentheism: belief that the world is contained within God or the divine.

pantheism: a philosophical or religious position that identifies the world and the divine.

pietism: a current in Protestant Christianity stressing personal religious experience and strict ethical behavior.

poststructuralism: a theoretical approach to texts which stresses that they are fields of signifiers without any determinate meaning, in which the "play of signifiers" is at work, and thus in which "meaning" is something arrived at, if at all, by the individual interpreter; includes "deconstruction."

scientism: an approach to understanding the world in which scientific modes of inquiry and notions of truth are the only ones acceptable; scientific positivism.

soteriocentrism: a distorted approach to theology that places the salvation of the individual as the central concern of God's relationship to the world.

teleology: the orientation of nature, history, or an individual life toward a final end or purpose. In scholastic terminology, final causality.

virtue ethics: ethical theory that stresses the habitual cultivation of the virtues, from which good ethical practices will follow. Distinguished from ethical theories stressing the priority of rules.

Womenchurch: a term popularized by Rosemary Radford Ruether in her book of the same name, referring to intentional communities of women who separate themselves "for a time" from mainstream churches, in order to discover and develop women's ways of worship and ecclesial community.

zeitgeist: literally, from the German, "the spirit of the time." The term is used to refer to the particular character or temper of a given period of history, the typical feeling or emotions that are "in the air" at any given time.

Index